X-LEE POETRY

An Outsider Inside

Verse and Rhymes from Post-Truth Times

A NOBLE GAS BOOK
Illuminating Minds For Design

A NOBLE GAS BOOK

Illuminating Minds For Design
noblegassuperior@gmail.com

Copyright © Lee Codrington 2025

FIRST EDITION

No part of this publication may be reproduced,
stored in a retrieval system, or transmitted in any form, or by any means
- electric, mechanical, photocopying, recording or otherwise -
without permission in writing, except for brief quotations
used in reviews, articles or scholarly work

All rights reserved

ISBN: 978-1-0369-3453-8

Book design by Yoc & X-Lee Poetry
Typesetting by Yoc

Printed and bound in Great Britain by
www.print2demand.co.uk

Impressions Creative Solutions, Huntingdon, UK

Contents

In Memoriam
Introduction
The Essential Ingredient

Sudden Twilight

I. HERITAGE & IDENTITY

Birth 3 – 5
The Song in My Heart 6 – 7
Social Media Post 8 – 11
Camouflage 12 – 13

II. SYSTEMS & INJUSTICE

Island of Strangers 15 – 16
Democratic Dictators 17 – 19
Cause & Effect 20 – 21
Fire In The Wheelie 22 – 24

III. TECHNOLOGY & DISCONNECTION

No Cash. No Cheques. No Standing Orders 26 – 27

Time for Joy 28 – 29

Time Zones 30

IV. ENVIRONMENTAL GRIEF

Ancient Wizened Oak 32 – 35

The Ark 36 – 38

Instant Night

I. IDENTITY & SELF-DISCOVERY

Took Me Swagger 41 – 46

Colourful Collaborators 47 – 49

Black Brown Paradox 50 – 51

Sanctuary of Our Locked Front Door 52 – 55

Young Kids 56 – 60

II. POWER & SOCIETY

Batman's Penguins 62 – 63

Kevlar 64 – 66

Our Doors 67 – 69

Dogs of War 70 – 71

Labour Shortages 72 – 73

Forty Seven 74 – 76

If We Capitalise 77 – 78

Alone - A Solitary Black Man 79 – 84

III. TRAGEDY & INJUSTICE

Grenfell 86 – 90

Two Child Cap 91 – 94

Are We Okay? 95 – 97

Superior Inferior 98 – 101

Freedom Of Speech 102

Mental Help 103 – 104

America 105 – 109

Distant Dawn

I. ECHOES OF HISTORY

Ancient Aborigines 112 – 114

1835 115 – 117

A Tribute To The Forgotten Soldiers 118 – 119

II. FACES OF INEQUALITY

Black Lives Matter 121 – 123

White & Cream 124 – 125

Taking The Knee 126 – 127

III. GENERATIONS IN CONFLICT

Intergenerational Strife 129 – 130
Roofs Over Heads 131 – 132

IV. CRISIS & HOPE

My Dear Deer 134 – 135
Carbon Credits 136 – 137
Pay 138 – 139

V. PERSPECTIVES OF LEADERSHIP

Decide 141 – 142
Arise From Your Slumber 143 – 144

Emerging in the Light - with Insight

I. IDENTITY & HERITAGE

X-Lee Poetry 147 – 151
Black 152 – 154

II. MEMORY & ACCOUNTABILITY

Lest We Forget 156 – 157

Leaders 158 – 160

III. AWAKENING & OPENNESS

Embrace the Strange 162 – 163
Hearts 164 – 165
Kindness 166 – 167

IV. VISION FOR THE FUTURE

Holistic Position 169 – 171
Master Your Destiny 172 – 174
Better Tomorrows 175 – 176

V. SELF & COLLECTIVE HEALING

Essential Love 178 – 180
Already Been 181 – 183
Kinetic Soup (A Prayer to Self) 184   187
Embodiment of Love 188 – 189

A Final Note

Wise Words Spoken 191
Gratitude 192

In Memoriam

This book is dedicated to the memory of my Beloved Grandfather, Julius Oliver Daly. No child could have wished for a kinder, gentler and more loving Grandfather. Few people could read and have the measure and understanding of others as you so quietly did. You were a beautiful and indelible example to us all. To know you was a privilege. To be your Grandson was the greatest gift! The words written on these pages have been inspired by you.

This book is also written and dedicated to the memory of my Grandmother, Muriel Ledgister. Everyday spent with you in Jamaica was a most wonderful joy. We spent too much time transatlantically apart. But in the very first moment that we met, my heart bloomed and danced to your tune. And in that instant I'd known and loved you all my life.

This book is further dedicated to the memory of my Idrin, Jamie Clark, whose sudden and untimely departure left everyone floundering in the dark. Your love and laughter illuminated our hearts. We were devastated to have lost you on this side of the veil. Yet so privileged to have had you brightening, enlightening and uplifting our lives.

You, me, and all ah we, remain forever a loving family!

Introduction: *An Outsider Inside*

This book is a rhyming monologue of passive observations centred on social, cultural, political, economic and environmental power struggles from the perspective of a second/third generation immigrant, born in Britain yet navigating life as an outsider, inside an unharmonious and disenchanted Dis-United Kingdom with her populace depressed, anxious and confused by poor politicians; entrenchment in an economic orthodoxy that serves only a small percentage of her people; has voluntarily encumbered herself with a unique set of crippling self-inflicted trade sanctions and tariffs; and has a significant part of its media set firmly in ideological stances disseminating post-truths. And in addition, she has also suffered further shocks and set backs over recent decades including the smashing of her worker's unions, privatisation of her state owned assets, de-industrialisation, deregulation, austerity and the COVID 19 pandemic.

Being in my fifties and almost eighty percent through my anticipated productive working lifespan, I am sure that I am not alone when I say that I have worked damn hard, yet I am still trying to get a start in life. How many of you have friends and peers who are still living with their parents? Have you had to turn to the bank of mum and dad to get on the property ladder? How many of you are still turning to your parents for loans or financial gifts, even though you may be married, own property [are mortgaged up to the eyeballs] and have children of your own? How many of you have zero or little savings and are still living payday-to-payday, even though you may well have a nice car on the driveway, wear designer clothing and have nice holidays or children attending private schools? How many of you have yet to achieve much, if any, of the above and are still fighting to keep the wolf from the door? I could go on....

I often feel like a teenager who is still trying to gain a foothold that may afford an ability to maintain, sustain and ultimately find that hallowed place of carefree financial comfort. I have a university degree. I have been a director of companies. I have done good work of which I have been very proud, yet not been paid, on too many occasions to mention. I have attended job interviews where the opening line of the interviewer has been "I am not going to give you the job." And I have applied for jobs, that I am adept and capable of doing, only to be told that my qualifications are obsolete or inappropriate, which in turn invalidates my experience. I have been invited to interview only to be told that I am over qualified to be considered. However, when working in the construction industry, no one ever told me I was over qualified to wield a shovel and dig holes. On the contrary, at times I was accused of being dishonest, incompetent and a whole host of other things which were unpalatable to bear, particularly when integrity, diligence and honesty are vitally important qualities to me. And did I mention, we are in the midst of a labour shortage.

My childhood was frequently punctuated with poignant greetings like "Fuck off back to Africa, Nig Nog!" And until the EU referendum, it was something to which I had given less of my attention. But I felt an acute level of distress when a friend told me about a child of European citizens that they knew, who had chosen to make Great Britain their home. Their child, like myself at a tender age, and so many others whose parents came to the UK from overseas, had barely if at all, known any other country but Great Britain as their home. But these children of European and migrant parentage were being made aware that they were now not welcome here, as I had so often been made to feel as a child, by other children, adults and politicians. Bringing such discomfort, anxiety, trauma and distress recklessly and needlessly to young souls was and is, in my view, unforgivable. The political class should have known better and should have behaved better, far far better. They are supposed to promote and uphold the highest of values and virtues for all residents and constituents, irrespective of nationality. Not race in search of the lowest.

The topics this book addresses and the views expressed, in the form of rhyming monologues exploring the difficulties in navigating away from the darkness and emerging with insight into the light, are in no way representative of anyone but the writer. They are passive observations of someone who has spent their whole life residing inside whilst being an incessant outsider to all, except to those by whom he is known and loved, within the country of his birth.

It is my sincere hope that in this work, you may find resonance and provocation for consideration.

The Essential Ingredient

The main and essential ingredient in the reading of a poem is you. Without your eyes or hands, if reading Braille, scanning the words written and turning the page, there is no verse or rhyme to be read or heard. There is no wrong or right way to read a poem, indeed the only thing that matters is that you are here to read. But it may enhance your interaction with, and satisfaction of, a poem if you imagine you are reading it aloud or, if you are able to, actually read it out loud and bring the magic of your ears into the fray.

Read a poem as if you are reading it to an enchanted audience or a crowd of friends and family who are delighted to hear your voice, and are hanging on to every word that you say. Let the words radiate as you orate, play with the emphasis of the syllables and if you wish to, allow for pauses and vary your cadence from fast to slow creating a diversity of pitch and tones, from high to low, as you uniquely flow, sending the words to your imaginary audience home. And as you do so, you will feel how your fluctuations and transformations will penetrate and resonate within your soul, making your experience of interacting with the poem more profound, compounding your enjoyment and inquisitiveness to further delve.

A sanctuary can be found in reading poems. New thought provocations and considerations can be found in reading poems. Comfort, peace and clarity can be found in reading poems. But don't ever forget or neglect to remember, that it is you who is the main and essential ingredient in the reading of a poem. Without you, words await patiently and silently in stasis because you are their catalyst, you are the oasis of a poets inviting writing, ready for your reading and reciting.

If you can, read a poem early in the morning when starting your day. It may serve as a daily meditation, a reassuring mantra or a beautiful incantation that sets you on your way. Later in the evening when peaceful moments have set in, or whilst you are sat on a train or a bus in the midst of the daily hubbub you can ignore all the fuss and make some space to just... Read a poem aloud to the inside of your mind and let your synapses spark, so your brain can shine regal delivering renewed warmth of joy to the chakra of your heart.

Read some poetry every day and allow them to lead your thoughts astray. Read a poem once, but better to read it again, twice. Take a poem out with you in your pocket, treasured like it has been concealed in an extra large secret locket then read it thrice, four times or five. And soon it will become and feel intimately nice, enticed and entwined with the very essence of your being. Reading poetry can be liberating and freeing, like it's your own special vice in which you can find a new word power to positively surprise, suffice and empower you in ways you previously never knew. Your special poem will fortify and edify you.

May I reiterate and remind you that you are the main and essential ingredient in the reading of a poem. Breathe the spirit of your life into words that in service to you are actually expedient. And in time, whether short or long, you will find in a poem merits that you are compelled to share with those around you, because you are unable to sequester the significance in words that loudly resound profound within you.

So read a poem whenever you can. Read a poem because the poem needs you, as only you, the main ingredient, will and can feel and completely understand as the pages of these words written rest in your hands.

Sudden Twilight

I. HERITAGE & IDENTITY

Birth

And so this is the period of gestation
You and I, we have all been there
And during this period there are many many incantations sung
For this is the season of excitement and anticipation
The rarefied air is filled with reverent adoration
And still, we are yet to arrive upon this Earth
For us, this is the unthinking and unknowing time
That precedes the moment of our arrival, our birth

All that we have felt is the steadiness and the stillness
Where the egg met the seed, and our embryo was formed
To develop safely ensconced in the womb
One day we shall leave this world of Terra Firma in a coffin, in a tomb
But hopefully that day is a very very long way off
And although this life is brief and fleeting, we have no idea of this

We have no idea of anything
Aside from the familiar syncopated rhythms of
Our mother's metronomic beating, and beautifully repeating biology
Where we unknowingly know the concealed world of the umbilical
And the womb
And one day we shall call her Momma, Mum or Mother
She shall be the only one
And by birth there will and never can be no other

Her waters are broken
In unison with the gravity of Mother Earth, nature has spoken
And now is our time to be consciously awoken
Spring has sprung

And we follow the passage of the water down to the well
But in here there is no time to luxuriate, to dwell
For we have entered the birthing canal to shortly be dispelled
On this day of our long anticipated and welcomed arrival
We get our first taste of Mother Earth

An assault, an invasion of countless new senses has begun
Intense pressures are applied to the whole of my body
And oddly, none of this discomfort has been of my choosing
Particularly the squeezing and compression, resulting in my bruising
My resistance is futile, this is a battle that I'm losing

Ice cold air descends like spectral blows, raining down on my skin
The warm hand of the midwife
And the embrace of my loving next of kin
There's a cacophony of loud muffle free noises
That sear my eardrums
Sounds of concern, of love, of laughter
Relief and joy, it's a girl, it's a boy

The brightness of the light burns my blurred,
Unfocussed and still unopened eyes
This is a most unwelcome and unpleasant surprise
With the first breath in my lungs my senses are stung
I exhale a first burst of air manifesting as an
Involuntary high pitched scream
Which again sears all the nerves of my newly awakened senses
And the relentless vacuum of inhalation
And exploding of my lungs has begun
And again I exhale a blast that assaults eardrums

And so this cycle shall now perpetuate
This is the impediment that life dictates

This overwhelming experience is a breach of the peace
And my peace has been inexplicably broken
And now that I am awoken to embark upon this un-chartered journey
Our previous equilibrium has been shattered, it is no more
Our previous peaceful equilibrium has been broken
And still I am not yet even two minutes old
And unknowingly I have so much to look forward to and behold
So now begins a new season as Spring has truly sprung
To Nurture new life
To grow and unfold our future stories yet to be written
And yet to be told.....

The Song In My Heart

When I first started school
my infant class teacher tried to erase
and extinguish the song in my heart
Smacking was allowed and it was a skill
in which she was expertly proud

The eroding of a little one's confidence
And so each day to school and along the way
in frightened unbending straight legged walks
silent in tension not a single utterance of talk
My unease screamed visually before me
Body language fully in restraint and recoil
an unsuccessful foil fraught from the inevitable impending

My dear mother read and comprehended my fear
She thought what is going on here?
This has to be dealt with
My cheerful son's sadness has to be ended
The song in his heart has to be mended
And uplifted from where it has descended

She steered a path clear to my teacher and asked
whether everything with me was okay in class?
And without hesitation my teacher proceeded to say
That with a different cultural background
things would be much much better for me
once I had learned how to speak English properly
and could make myself understood...
In English

My mother was dumbfounded angered and offended
She went straight to see the headmaster
and voiced her concerns about my teachers predispositions
You see, I only spoke one language clearly and freely
And that language was the same as that of all my school friends
The headmaster said that my teachers position
was one that he could not defend
or even pretend to comprehend

To this day, I don't know whether my teacher was fired
or submitted her resignation by demand
But I never saw or was fraught by her ever again
The hateful teacher was gone, and for this five year old
the rotten and intimidating days were soon forgotten
and a new happiness was soon begotten
And after a distressing beginning
the song in my heart was again at a start

Social Media Post

This person I knew
Shared a post on a host, a social media channel
Disparaging the Black Lives Matter campaign
With claims only made to inflame
Ignite and incite anger and fear

It brought defamation of my people too close
The post chose to slander Brown skinned people
Who looked like me, my friends and our families

I read the post twice
I read the post twice
Incredulous I was disappointed
For the post it was not nice

It wasn't for me
Yet it was about me
And I took this shit personally
I thought I'm not having this
You're taking the piss

Purporting that we have no issue
With institutional racism or racists
That we are the trouble
That we were a source of criminality, and all societies ills
That we have no cause to complain, and so we should refrain
Like our campaign had no foundation
Or valid grounds to be found
And would only end in vain

The post claimed that we were murderers, and rapists
And much more than I could list
But, you get the gist

Unusually, I responded
Writing to the sharer on their social media feed
I tried to sow a seed and a shared a little story
And trust me
This ain't no Jackanory

It's 1976 and I'm four years old
The summer was super hot
The ground was scorched
But this tale is cold

When I played on the street
Amidst the summer heat
A neighbour would step out of his front door
And looking in my direction
He would proudly stand to attention
And raise his arm aloft

In the street it was just him
And little four year old me
Accompanied by his sieg heil salute frequently
I didn't understand what was brewing
But I knew it wasn't friendly
Yet he was performing this especially for me
At me, and for only me to see

Innocently I asked my mother
What his gesture was all about?
And she had to point out

That my skin was beautifully Brown
And this clown, his skin was cream
And in his mind this meant that he had every right
To frighten and be terribly mean to me
Because I was beautifully Brown and not his cream
I did not belong to his team

In the years that elapsed
At times I wondered just how my mother felt
As she spelt it out, and was forced to explain
This new reality to the four year old me
Her precious klein Lee

In the end, I got it
I couldn't accept it or come to respect it
Because it hurt
And this dude, he was my friends dad
Mad!

One morning I stood looking in the mirror
Smiling approvingly
I inspected, cream pyjama top in hand
Brown pyjama trousers in the other
Smiling approvingly I liked them both equally

I appreciated both components of the pyjama set
I saw no threat, and could not distinguish
Reasons for one to be diminished for the other
In status to be elevated, segregated

I politely posted my reply
I posted a version of this story
On their social media feed

And indeed, they came off platform
To message me privately

Where amongst other things, they said
"Oh Lee, I am so sorry you were offended
For being mistaken and greeted
As German!"

Camouflage

It is no coincidence
that the words camouflage
and sabotage rhyme

Sometimes when we are in fear
we try to hide
we try to camouflage
who we are

And actually
what we are doing
is sabotaging
who we are

We camouflage to hide
and then we cannot show
who we are
to the world

And therefore
we go missing
but not only
are we missing out
on experiences

The world is missing
what we have
to offer

Camouflage
is self-sabotage
And self-sabotage
is the worst form
of camouflage

II. SYSTEMS & INJUSTICE

Island of Strangers

I am upset
I am frustrated
The PM says I am no longer to be tolerated
For I am a danger
I am a stranger on the island where I was born

I am increasingly scorned
Because of ideologies revisited, redefined
And spawned in new acceptable forms
To which Brown and Black Kings and Queens
And children blessed with melanin tones like me
Can never, will never, perceptibly conform

How are you to distinguish whether I am native born?
How are you to distinguish whether I am native born?

The PM is trying to snatch new votes
He now promotes policies against me
Progressive or reductive
Destructive or constructive
Collectivist or Separatist
The PM insists he is listening
He understands and that he now gets it

A renewed wind increasing
Once upon a time I dared to think
It was decreasing, receding
And going out like the tide
Yet in the back of my mind

I have always been knowing
That white pride would be back
That the Black and Brown you like
Are alright
It's all the other unknown non-whites

You want removed from your sight
Better still extradited, severed and deported
From residing on these fine hallowed shores
Targeted scores in tens of thousands
In silence erased, unheard, never again to be seen

Footnote:

Poem written as a reply to: "Island of Strangers" Speech given by Prime Minister Sir Keir Starmer Migration White Paper press conference on 12th May 2025

Democratic Dictators

How can this be a free
And truly autonomous Parliamentary Democracy
When MPs are whipped into making voting decisions
Irrespective of the wants, will, needs, voices, or perspectives
Of the constituents who elected
And voted them in as their representative
In the Houses of Parliament?

How can this be a free
And truly autonomous Parliamentary Democracy
When the party leadership dictates
What their MPs may or may not say
On a multitude of morals, principles and issues of the day
It makes for a mockery, a tissue of lies
For not every elected member
Will share the views the PM's vanguard eyes
Has selected, as prized, prioritised

How can this be a free
And truly autonomous Parliamentary Democracy
When MPs are banished and frozen
From their parties chosen
For voting with conscience and clear hearts
Representing the concerns of their constituencies
With sincerity and authenticity
Rather than from a place of conflicted duplicity?

How can this be a free
And truly autonomous Parliamentary Democracy

When Cabinet Ministers have little or no agency
To shape their departments
Or influence the direction of governance
Through collective consensus?

How can this be a democracy at all
When corporations and private equity firms
Have the government's ear
Dictating deregulation and 'light-touch' law
Over that of policies to benefit the peoples
Of this land and other nations, rightfully as equals?

How can this be a free and fair democracy
When too many people are left behind
Treated as insignificant and maligned
Having their access to welfare
And Human Rights eroded
Whilst corporates and hedge funds
In their activities reap subsides,
Tax breaks and protections
Encrypted, encoded
In laws they help design

It is beyond time for us all
To call out this era by its name
A hyper individualistic, capitalistic regime
Destroyers of sovereign institutions, apparatus of state
Where dismantlers are despots on the take
Leaving only devastation in their wake
Tsunamis, earthquakes
Of social collapse

They must be resigned

And economies, democracies
Must be redefined, redesigned
Inclusive by design
Serving the Earth first
And all humankind

Cause & Effect

Bad calls, worse responses, legitimised
To ligate an instance of existence
With an insistence of extreme courses of resistance

Results of effects adverse
Harming those they are meant to serve
And protect
Briefly pausing, then causing
A recourse to resourcing desperate measures
To organise, reject, address, and publicly disrespect

Denials of fair minded access
To healthcare, to welfare
To other responsibilities of the State

Accusing foreigners
British citizens lazy, disabled, insane, and crazy
Deplorables and **dishonourables** amidst this society
Invisibles. Irregular arrivals upon these shores
All of whom **are no respectables priority**

Cause and effect:
Vexed, knee-jerk reflexes excitedly
Inviting fair ground reflections
Ill-advised sanctions, seizures
Refracted failures redacted

Indiscriminate displeasures mounting
Discounting protecting the innocent

The vulnerable, and needy

"How can they be in poverty, and lacking
Yet have the knack
To satiate their greedy?"

Flaunting an affluence
Overriding their needy:
Mobility cars, tattoos, smart phones and flat-screen TVs

Even this Government's raising of funds
Is shameless and seedy
Fiscal Rule fundamentalism doesn't render you blameless
When you're literally punishing the poor
Wringing them out for more

Cause and effects affect you and yours
Cold, behind closed doors
Empty mouths silenced
Locked jaws

Fire In The Wheelie

The four richest people in Great Britain
Have more wealth than 20 million Britons

The richest fifty families have 466 Billion
In Wealth
When the wealth of all the rest
Of Great Britain
Is 466 Billion

The richest one percent
Have more wealth than seventy percent
Of Britain's citizens

Yet for the best of Great Britain
The nation is smitten
With the most liberal and lax of tax laws
For the richest of all
Of its most treasured beneficiaries of state

Great are these highly pleasured residents
Treated and respected as rightful tax relief
Dependants, resplendent
To cater favourably for independent wealth generators
Essential as presidential economic invigorators

Today Britain's multi-millionaires
Are empowered, glowingly flowered
And are on their way to becoming,
For those that are not already there,

Billionaires

And for the benefit of the poor
When it comes to billionaires
This country needs many many, many many
Many many more

But you the unemployed and working poor
You want your country back
So whitey's riot riot attack attack
Fire in the wheelie attack attack

From Asian, Brown, mixed, and black
You want to take your country back

Thought you already took border control
And your sovereignty back
Fire in the wheelie attack attack
Bricks through windows
Attack attack

Refugees in hotels holed up attack attack
For unending spells attack attack
Asylum seekers prevented from working, attack attack
Stuck here living in a limbo, attack attack

Migrant hate, the media profit and sell
Government policies magnify and propel
Riot riot attack attack
Fire in the wheelie attack attack

Did you know the first Great Britons
Before Great Britain was called Britain
Had jet hair black and brown skin back
Before fire in wheelies attack attack

Could it be that these people
These refugees in boats
Are your direct ancestors coming right back
Returning home
To reclaim ancestral thrones
Bricks through windows, attack attack

Blighty's Whiteys attack attack
Fire in the wheelie attack attack
From Asian, Brown, mixed, and black
You want to take your country's wealth back

So long as there's
Asian, Brown, mixed, and Black
Is there not another way
To have an even distribution
Of this nation's wealth back?

At a cost of £2 per taxpayer per year
For people fleeing war and tragedy
And coming right here
What the hell is there to fear?

Footnote:

Together With Refugees - "A Bill at What Price?"
Published February 14th, 2022

III. TECHNOLOGY & DISCONNECTION

No Cash. No Cheques. No Standing Orders

For me?
The multi-national corporation
The buyer of publicly owned companies
Sold off in privatisations -
Exclusive monopolistic actors
across regional and national markets
were highly desirable investment factors

As were the knock-down sale prices
for the fattest of cakes
with the most stupendous of slices

Potential for profit? Undeniable
Revenue streams? Increasing, unquantifiable
Government subsidies? Essential and viable
And vitally, for me, they are free

Especially, if I raise
the looming threat of "Trade winds in adversity"
And invoke that most majestic of terms:
Redundancies
Then in will flow
more of those subsidies
To be consumed by our shareholders
voraciously
in varying degrees

For you?
Access to my services and produce

Costs good money
To be paid by Direct Debit only, I'm afraid

No cash
No Cheques
No standing orders

Time For Joy

Where is time for joy
If you allow so little time
That all that you can see and hear
Is negative noise

Where is time for joy
If you put yourself
Under so much pressure
That you have no time for leisure

Where is time for joy
When you rush rush rush
And have no space to think clearly
And crave only the hush of silence

Where is time for joy
When you are always running late
And you are unable to appreciate
The love
The kindness and generosity around you
That is abundantly great

Where is the joy
When your body is flushed
With stress and cortisol
Eroding the goodness of your soul

Where is time for joy
If you will not slow

And be calm

Where is the joy
If you will not dial down
The alarm
Where is the joy
In self-inflicted mental harm

Where is time for joy
When your only relaxation
Is running yourself into evisceration

Where is the joy
And charm
That magnetically drew friends
To you close
Before you became so miserable
Impatiently self-absorbed
And Morose

Time Zones

We scan the unacceptable
on our phones
Desensitised and lacking
in the required empathy perceptible

In the comfort of our homes
there is no competition
in the mission for attention
loyalty and affection

Secure in the company of loved ones
the technological world
forever unfurled
isolates us and renders us strangely alone

Physically together
yet in different time zones
We touch the same screens
But not the same soul
Scroll past pain
But never feel whole

IV. ENVIRONMENTAL GRIEF

Ancient Wizened Oak

Silence is broken by the dawn chorus, and our senses are awoken
by footsteps of foraging hedgehogs, squirrels, hares and deers
the tranquillity of nomadic tribes in passing
with grazing sheep and goats and cows and horses
We used to hear the whispers of the animal kingdom
and the gratitude of your gracious voices

You lived around I, my kind and we
We cohabited and you lived freely amongst us, and we were all free
You see, my father was born in 1373
And when I came along in 1564, he said we all couldn't make it
because things were much different then
when compared to way back when he was born
and was fortunate enough to break out of acorn

Surrounded by family, I was schooled a great change was afoot
Rage and despair had settled in the air and in the soil
the busy fungi and mycelium communicated
frantically they worked and toiled
and I listened to the rumours as sap now hissed and boiled

We were under attack without any means to strike back
The adolescent me wondered, what is this attack
and how can it be so bad?
And each time I asked, I drove my living ancestors mad
They said it was just too bad that youths like me would never understand
before the impending decimation of
Our beautiful ancestral forested lands
By these once dependent but now marauding regiments

and bands of people with their ill-intended hands

And then in 1723 the long held rumours became our reality
just as I was pushing up high and breaking through the great canopy
murderous people came into our forest and began
hacking and whacking, attacking my brothers and sisters
my cousins and their grandmothers, and countless others

And these murderous people they ignored
our screams, they ignored our pleas
They wielded the saw and the axe with unrelenting force
indiscriminate, genocidal, with no remorse
They cleared vast areas, vast vast previously unimaginable tracks
and as we were cut, chopped, culled and killed
we all died inside as our great friend fungi screamed, wailed and cried
for us and with us, as soon many of their kind too, died
And soon much water pooled and once stable soils began to slide
and the animals and pollinators in droves
they too died, as did so many of you
and just like all our friends we came to despise you, too

We became your new source of capital
a commodity to trade for food and shelter, for you and your brood
We became new weapons in wars unseen before
We became hulls and masts of ocean going ships
carrying human cargoes to a world anew with no return
We became props in mines and excavation shields in tunnels
We became sleepers for rails and cut and cover channels
We inhabited lock gates in rivers and canals
and graced her waters afloat as narrow boats

Have you forgotten that we blessed this Earth?
It is our roots that broke rock and turned it to soil

Have you forgotten that it was from our natural decomposition
that you derived coal and oil?
Have you forgotten that we store and capture carbons
and cool the air in Mother Earth's environs?
Have you forgotten that we nourish you with our life giving oxygen?

For one hundred and fifty nine years I lived in the shade
and just as I was graduating to the unhindered sun grade
to stand for five hundred years in a grand and joyous parade
to hear the clarity of the windy leaf serenade
to photosynthesise in the fine canopy glade
I had begun to share the sky with my compatriot trees on high

Now only I one remain, in this bare field
A land otherwise emptied of tree life
once a forest full off the busy-ness of nature's
life thriving, but now empty
From my ten million acorns barely any spawn
from which there are no ancient oaks to ever be born
This decline has rapidly become a frightening new norm
And for my father, mother, brothers, sisters, friends
and all familial others, I am still bereaved and forlorn

For the dawn chorus that was, is no more
and there is no peace and silence to be enjoyed as before
just an escalating mechanical violence
and ever expanding roads, motorways and screaming planes
to be heard from afar
with their polluting exhausts burning my leaves
and obscuring the stars
and noxious pollutants of progress that poison my roots

And just when I think it cannot get any worse
inevitably I am to be uprooted with chainsaw and stump grinder
to make way for an exclusive gated residential estate
where the risk of my toppling on to a proposed new roof
is deemed to be just too great

And for this giver of oxygen
a capturer of carbon, a maker of soil
and a harbinger or Nature's Children vital
this is such a sorry sorry state
for a tree so humble and so so great!

The Ark

I stepped through the veil
With a pail full of life-giving elixir
The sun, the moon, the stars, fully eclipsed
Time slowed, the force of gravity, and the soil erode
Tides arose, and the still air froze
Levitating, a snail ate a frog

The sea consumed the lake, and the earth began to quake
Frantically, I sought shelter, from this frightening helter-skelter
With pairs of bears, bison, chimpanzee, and deers
I sheltered with sparrow-hawks, whales, sharks, and vultures
Amongst these, there was even plants, vegetation, and trees

And in varying degrees of gruff growls
Barks, pops, chirps, squeals, and squawks, they said:

"Glad to see you haven't brought a harpoon or gun
Your weaponry is anything but heavenly
Especially for me, us, he, she, and we
Welcome to our ark; herein you will find
All of Earth life's divine and vital sparks

You see, humankind, you are living crazy
In this perfect planetary park
And because you're too lazy to find a way out of your crazy
We are waiting here, sheltering in this ark

You need to recognise your fundamental part at the heart
Of the chaos that you are sowing

There is an animal extinction endangering all life familial
A land, air, and sea dereliction that is growing

You understand and you are knowing
Of the devastation from the seeds that you are cultivating
Yet still sowing

So we are sitting this one out in this ark
Large Hadron Collider, and you think you're so smart
You think that your fire rockets and technology
Will enable you to depart this perfect planetary paradise
This earth
For a new restart on a planet apart, inhospitable but anew

But whatever you do, success will measure comparably few
You think you can terraform a new norm
To make a new world appropriate to sustain
For a species with such big brains
You are vain and completely deranged

We are sitting out this one
We are waiting in this ark for you to end what you've begun

Otherwise your life will beget us our death
And with each oxygen-fading abuse and breath
Your life be-gets you your death

There are obvious solutions for our freedom
And your freedom to live and thrive
Alive in harmony and with vitality

But that can happen only
If you can escape your manufactured, phoney

Synthetic, pathetic, grandiose illusions

Until then, we animals, plant life, vegetation
Fish, insects, microbes, and birds
We will wait patiently within this ark
For the many many months and years
Of war followed by the dark
Preceded by that unintended
But inevitable, succession of nuclear sparks
And the vacuum that left zero room for error
Other than for your life to be-get your death

And in your death is our new birth
In your death, we will be free to draw fresh breath
And breathe a sigh of relief

For once you are gone
Again we will inherit, love, respect, and cherish our Earth
The sun, the moon, the stars
The air, the sea, and the land will once again
And safely be ours"

And with that, they relieved me of my pail of live-giving elixir
Then nudged me out from the safety of their ark, their shelter
Back into the chaos of the frightening helter-skelter

Instant Night

I. IDENTIFY & SELF-DISCOVERY

Took Me Swagger - A Windrush Story

You took me swagger
Invite me to this here mother land
Where every thing
And every thing British is grand
Where electric light is on demand

And here I stand
In this here strange land
Where they eat chips and fish
On newspaper print instead of dish

Bathe in a large tin pot
About once a week
And finding toilet in cold yard
Is a hard game of hide and seek

Is the truth me ah speak
And man it is bleak
Enough of them can't read
And say they can't understand
The Queen's English that me speak

And here I stand
A proud Black West Indian African
British citizen
Educated and anointed in all things grand
From this here motherland

I am both surprised and disappointed

That British ladies and gentlemen
Did not know, care
Or understand anything about me, us, and we
Or their varied and numerous colonies

From whence we came
For perpetual revolutions of the earth
Upon the union flag
The sun, it never set, or arose

And here I stand froze
In this strange land
Where at work they call me "Oi"

I say
"That is not my name"

Him say then she say
"It don't matter Blackie
You all look the same"

And so we warriors became soldiers
Bus drivers, and nurses
Engineers, and undertakers loading hearses

African warriors, we became musicians
And poets, educators, and scholars
In the name of progress, and integration
A whole generation of families broken
Tragically, transatlantically

For the rebuilding of this here mother nation
So many of our children never knew

The majesty of their grandparents

Others for the longest of time
Barely knew their own parents, or siblings

So much sacrifice
Selfless, courageous, and sacred
To make a better life in the service
Of this place, this fine green land
Full of love and hate, at an equal rate

This land, the mother country
Where with loud exhalations
Some of my British peers don't want me

Enoch Powell cried out about
Us soon to be holding the whip hand
And city streets soon
To run with rivers of blood

In a 1964 by-election
Since the last war, Smethwick
Had been a safe labour seat

Peter Griffiths, the Tory candidate
Ran a campaign, based on race hate:
*"If you want a nigger for a neighbour
Vote Labour."*

This Tory, he came with a caustic story
That made white people feel sweet
So they elected him

To the parliamentary seat

Not before the Teddy Boys
With their white iron bars
And the ascendancy
Of Kelso Cochrane's spirit
To the sun the moon
And eternal peace
In the stars

All for trying to make a life
In this, the mother country
Where there are few men gentle
And the people them are mental

Sixty years and more we prevail
Irrespective of assails
And after sixty years
No more faithful a service

Now you are deporting me
All because I've no longer a valid passport
You see you are singling me out
Disproportionally

Disparaging me, for we
Are no longer welcome
In this here, hostile environment

Seldom has a nation
Had at it's hand
So much blood and sufferation
To behold

My peoples honour
Scholars manuscripts of truth
Wisdom and glories untold, are known
But buried in vaults, and yet to be told

You see this is my land
This is my world
Built by the blood of my veins
That stains your hand
And drove an industrial revolution
In ah this land

Sugarcane toil
Of my ancestors
Remember British man
You are my descendants
And you were my dependants

I came here first
Before this nation ever existed
I colonised the whole earth
I wrote ancient scriptures, hieroglyphics
And painted cave pictures

I embedded the constellations
Of the stars upon this earth
I sailed the seven seas
And scaled the highest peaks

I studied the seasons, the plants, and the trees
I reasoned with the animals

The fish, the birds, and the bees
In harmony with nature
I cured all disease
I invented your religions
Gave you philosophy
Freedom of thought, mediation
And meditation

I gave you words to be spoken
And yet, you still stole my swagger
Branded you pack it up in a bag ah
And try to sell it back I'ah

I gave you words to be spoken
I gave you Jazz, Blues, Rock, Reggae, and Hip Hop

And yet you still stole my swagger
Branded you pack it up in a bag ah
And try to sell it back I'ah

Well this black, this black I swagger is real
Yeah you don't know the deal
And you don't know how I feel

Footnote:

References Shadow Secretary of State, Enoch Powell's "Rivers of Blood" Speech, April 20th, 1968
Kelso Cochrane was killed in a racially motivated murder, in Notting Hill, May 17th, 1959. (a week after the Notting Hill Riots).
https://committees.parliament.uk/writtenevidence/12263/html

Colourful Collaborators

The art of being adaptable
being applauded for belonging to an exclusive club
only the best of shoulders rubbed
in circles rarefied and exclusive
Being forthright and conclusive in conviction
championed as true Brits with true grit
loyal and all for it
without conflict and contradictions
spoken derelictions

Bringing forth unspeakable and unpalatable truths
advocating for the wholly unacceptable
for you are the exception
as a visionary you are perceptible
of problems forthcoming
that no one but you can see

You can speak for the benefits of segregation
the problems and failures caused by integration
and your words cannot be interpreted as racism bare faced
when spoken excitedly by Black and Brown politicians
who have served as cabinet ministers
at the heart of Government

If the message that is racist as meant
is spoken in the media, written and sent
by Brown and Black skinned journalists and politicians
they know our customs for they are British
they are us, they are exceptions set apart from the rest

who rightly and justifiably consider themselves
the absolute and exceptional best

Degrading and dehumanising their own
abroad and at home
making fools of themselves
thinking that they are the braves
Yet they are themselves blind
and enslaved to the depraved manipulators

Who have brainwashed them
and fed them unconscionable lines
to be spoken about people
who are needlessly suffering in the worst of times

They believe they have no connection
to their ancestry, their history
better, separate
segregated from their own stories

And singing the racists song
singing the sexists and the misogynists song
waving the nationalists banner
but seen still
as Black and Brown
immigrants

As Jonny & Jenny Foreigner
and anything but British
irrespective of their enthused espousals
eliciting cheers and approving arousals

They are just useful vehicles
to carry a despicable message
whose egos are pampered for parades
as the Right wingers charade
racing only for the bottom

Where all to be found is rancid
and rotten

Black Brown Paradox

When I looked in the mirror
I saw a handsome, happy boy

But when you saw me
You only saw a colour
Unintelligent, unfeeling
Incapable of understanding
Or fulfilling
What you were demanding

You only saw Brown
You only saw Black
You shouted insults at me
Quick, I answered you back
For being "disruptive and insolent"
I came under attack

Struck verbally
With your vociferous hyperbole
And with both sides of your hands
Front and back

And I couldn't fight back
Resist and repel your attacks

Back in the days
When four year olds
Teachers could smack
and physically attack

And no one fought back

Sanctuary of Our Locked Front Door

Two brothers heading home from Thursday club
On a dark winters night, guided by sodium lights
We, the eldest of my two brothers and me
Are almost at our front door, calm and relaxed

It's just another Thursday
And our lane is deathly quiet, all the same

When suddenly
We are swept off our feet
By the force of a hurricane

We only knew the pain that comes through fear
Present in the moment
Like a deer under predation

Carried through a gap in the hedge
Taken beyond bramble and bushes
By these two mad mooshes
Clad in combats and Ballys

Panicked, I didn't dally
Lashing out with fists
Flailing legs and knees
My elbows were flying
Convinced any moment I'd be dying

But to live
I was trying, hard

And throughout the whole thing
I was crying, hysterically

When your feet can't touch the ground
And you are at the mercy of grown men
Big men

Who can carry you like a rag doll
And fend off your blows
Like a feather being blown

And all that you know is the certainty of this unknown:
If only we could just get home

Then through the intense struggle
One of the men laughed as he spoke

"Calm down calm down, it's just a fucking joke!"

Him and his mate were in their late teens
But me and my bro, we were just little boys
I wasn't even eight
I was in a hell of a state

And what we'd just experienced
Was a weight

Relieved
Neither me nor my brother spoke
We were too choked
To conjure a word

We just walked home

To and through
The sanctuary of our locked front door

Hanging up our coats
Feeling the warmth of the fire's welcoming roar

Mum asked
"Do you want a cup of tea?"

We instantly replied
"Yes please."

Pleased to be home
Safe behind the sanctuary
Of our locked front door
Just us four
Safe in harmony together
And free from harm, once more

Neither I nor my brother
Ever breathed a word
To my mother, or one another
About the mad mooshes
In combats and Ballys

We just parked and buried
A trauma, frightening and absurd
Where we fought for our lives
And then got on with our lives

Forty one years later
We spoke about it for there first time

I asked my brother, Keith

> *"Do you remember that night*
> *walking home from Thursday Club*
> *When those two men jumped us on the street*
> *And swept us off our feet?"*

> *"Yeah, I remember"*

My brother replied.
> *"I thought they were gonna kill us!"*

A long buried trauma
Safe behind
The sanctuary
Of our locked front door.

Young Kids

Young kids attending school
Want to look cool so dem ah play the fool
Break every rule to be cooler than cool
But you're a to yourself
Who you impressing?
You think you're living large
But your life is what you're messing

You're fessing' to be big
And you're fessing' to be bad
Distressing your parents
No lesson you do learn
You're just another kid who thinks
Why learn when you can earn easy monies
To be a rich boy and check plenty, plenty honeys

Then you get into trouble with the police
Dem ah can't burst you're bubble
You're just another kid in trouble
Cautioned you get a slap on the wrist
An easy release feeling dissed
You're pissed, after a night in the cell
Cold as hell, who cares
Oh well

You don't care
Undeterred your life is fair
You ah gwan for the top
At a pace no one can stop

People say one day you'll drop
Suffer a nasty shock
You think you're solid as a rock
Never shall you drop

As a child
You always promised yourself
Never to do shit work for anybody else
Never to be exploited and treated like a yes man
To dirty your hand for any other man

Now
This ideology I must analyse
My analogy of this means I cannot criticise
But where is the prize
For your gracious intellect?
Where did you consecrate your surplus energies?
Into negative vice I do believe

You got deeper into crime
Through rhyme I'm telling the story
Of how you are now doing time
You started teefing and selling bikes
From which the monies you did likes
Then you moved on to cars
Chilled and cruised with your spars

You liked a smoke, enjoyed a good toke
But now you're broke, all your monies gone
Too much smoke on tick
Then your dealer proclaimed

"Where's my money sonny?

I give you nuff smoke
When you gonna pay me?"

So you robbed an old lady
In front of the Old Bailey

Then you started selling dope
But the profits weren't enough
Then you moved onto coke and life was less tough

But even that didn't work with only one slight quirk
To much of that went up your nasal track
It made you slack back
Then you started smoking crack
And your life was wack

"What a waste of a good life"
Your mother and brother did say
"But him commit the crime
and him must pay the price"

For you lived your life
On streets of torment and strife
You used to carry a blade
Then its usefulness did fade
Full of self-importance
You thought everyone wanted to kill ya
So you got yourself a shooter
Became ghetto boy trooper

What did you do with your intellect?
Why did you buck up on your own self-respect?
You stopped thinking positive

Regressed instead of progressed
Heck you blatantly refused to put your life in check

Then another crack-dealer
Had the obstinate audacity
The intolerable incapacity
To start selling on your turf
So you told him he had a nerve
But the boy him get vex
And him try to break your neck

So you emptied your piece
Bo! Bo! Bo!
Dust the yoot like fleece
Fast you went to ground
Absolutely silent you never made a sound
By the police you were found

Now you're doing the prison circuit
At Her Majesties pleasure
One of many a judgemental error
Deprives you of leisure

Now you're doing bird
And you're doing big-up bird
Absurd are the past
Where you lived your life fast
Twenty three hours in a cell
Each day is purely hell
Still there's plenty dope and coke
Time is longer than rope

Still on the outside nothing has changed
My yoot-man kill up yoot-man
Ah live for the crack man
Unable to take stock
For dem ah hooked on the rock

Ending up in the dock
To live their futile lives
Under key and lock, man
Afar from the top
Under key and lock
Afar from the top

II. POWER AND SOCIETY

Batman's Penguins

Big Men do big deals
In a world that can barely contain them
In a world that they run
Yet think will be better off done and over
Should they ever see their own setting sun
And know that their time is coming near to be gone

When the vitality of their irrepressible sparks
Succumb to mortality
And a fear of the dark that lurked in their hearts
Instantaneously embarks
Encumbered with their Souls to encounter God's light
In full sight, sound and final analysis
To know their sins as only Big Men knew
But pretended they didn't know, sanction or do
To their incalculable victims

Big men do big deals
In a world that can barely contain them
Agree or disagree you must do as they please
Otherwise they will put you in a bind
The kind that will put you in an uncompromising squeeze
The dis-pleaser's windpipe and airflow needlessly seized
A stagnation of inhalation and exhaling breeze
Which once you did with thoughtless ease
Suspended, upended, unable to sneeze

So you do not oppose them
The Big Men that do big deals

For their Earthly God like power is real
They are not here to help or to heal
But it may be possible for you to cut a deal
So get in line or be road kill
Get in line or be road kill

Get the fuck in line
Or else it will be your blood that's spilling
Willing tyres distributing your regions and limbs
At Big Mens whims
Reprehensible yet unquenchable

This is a brave new era, and it begins right now
The era of Strong Men, Hard Mean
The muscular fat and lard men
Standing as dividers, deniers, deriders and Papal Kings
This is a brand new era
Of Gold plated, nuclear sequins
As Batman's Penguins

Kevlar

Kevlar
Kevlar the protective selection
For ruffling feathers
Kevlar the perfect protector
In times when truth that is granular
Inevitably, gradually filtering through
Like the polarity of gravity upon hourglass

The truth cannot forever be denied
Opposing voices cannot perpetually be decried
The truth cannot be forever hidden
Even from those who were blind and smitten
And invested in you all that they had
Paternal as their dad

Until even the most loyal
Of cultists, disciples, devotees
Are no longer able to deny their displeasure
Are no longer able to hide their surprise
Their disappointment at the gargantuan deceptions
Concealed in your lies
Abundantly broken before their once-unseeing eyes

They hung on as their neighbours lost jobs
They felt conflicted, they felt at odds
But aside from rising prices
They felt that these difficulties were unpleasant necessities

Even when the cousins of their colleagues and in-laws

Ended up in a Salvadorian penitentiary
Never again to be free

But it was okay because they believed
If the Sunny uplands were ever to be reached
Unpleasant necessities had to be breached
So they hung on as essential services were withdrawn
And then came the day when the business closed
And the spectre of redundancies arose
And they lost their own house

And quiet like a church mouse
The falsehood of the great lie crept home
Untruths belied in lies gnawed at their bones
Ties in which they were so convinced
That they were prepared to kill, in your gift
They were prepared to die for you
Victims of your grift to falsely uplift

They were prepared to do life without parole for you
And face down the lethal injection
Undertake another insurrection
And why?
For your lies

Certain that you would come to their rescue
Just like previous hostages
Insurrectionists evading evidence and justice
Having sentences annulled
Irrespective of threats, deaths and crushed skulls

This is the Kevlar hour
Essential and vital survival factors

For 47's loyalists
Yet more so for your detractors
Un-American actors

And vital for you
In the light of your mighty betrayal
Of those who fought for you
Risked it all for you
To lose it all because of you

Tooth and nail
Scatter gun rounds and bullets flail
And only Kevlar can protect
When the masses reject
Become your nemesis and get
Your gross deceit and depravity
Of which for so long
They were so gratefully in receipt

Only Kevlar can protect
When upon 47 Don, the truth avails

Our Doors

Our doors are open
Our doors are always open
We love a good human story
Especially one of hope that isn't too gory
Where our help and assistance means
We can bask in our glory

But can you not appreciate that on your behalf
Against despots and tyrants
We have spoken, warred, and broken their regimes
And our doors are open for negotiation and dialogue
And whether sincere or token
We have supported fledgling and established democracies
And where necessary we have provided training and weaponry
For the benefit of your safety, your security, your peace, and harmony
We have invested in, and supported quasi-governments, financially
For your and our convenience, with at times deviance
Irrespective of whether they are or are not morally broken
So please listen carefully to these words about to be spoken

Please know that it is unrealistic
Unreasonable and far too simplistic for you to think
That just because you are starving
That just because you have been tortured and raped
That just because your family members have been killed
By religious extremists, and things are beyond out of shape
That just because there is a power vacuum
That is voraciously consuming all compassion and normality
That just because there is a fog of war

Terraforming new and shifting realities
Amidst fire-fights, bombs and constant shelling
That's disassembling the once beautiful villages, towns
And cities in which you were dwelling
Where frightened families and children are silently yelling
Where the numbers of collaterals are continually swelling
In part as a result of the armaments
Upon which we are capitalising and selling

Please know that we know, that you are just smelling
An opportunity, without a real and valid reason
To leave your country, to leave your community

Please know that we know, that you are just smelling
An opportunity, without a real and valid reason
To leave your country, to leave your community

And remember prior to and before you flee
To bring your passports, and fill out all your paperwork
And visa applications properly
And enter our country, our territory legally
Otherwise you will be an economic migrant, here illegally
And you will be classed as anything, except a real and genuine refugee

And we will make every clever endeavour
To deport you back to where you came
Instead of having you sponging off us here
Where you don't belong

We don't care for your experience, qualifications and skills
Or the contribution you wish to make to our society
Our priority is a quasi-cutting of bills
Except in the safety of Rwanda

Where UK tax payer cash abundantly spills
Even if it means you have to lose your life, and limbs
We cannot acquiesce to your deceitful whims

Just know that we are not a soft touch
But there is one caveat that we will appreciate much
If you have access to the equivalent of two million pounds sterling
And you transfer that amount or more, into a UK bank
To be frank, your investment visa is already as good as stamped
Rest assured, you are most welcome here
And we wouldn't wish you anywhere else
Irrespective of passport and paperwork we'll waive you through
Things will be lovely and dandy and just fine for you

Our doors are open
Our doors are always open
We love a good human story
Especially one of hope that isn't too gory
Where our help and assistance means
We can bask in our good, generous, Christian principles, and glory
We stand ready to embrace you and your story

Footnote:

Poem written prior to the Tier 1 Investor Visa being abolished, on February 17th, 2022
https://researchbriefings.files.parliament.uk/documents/CBP-9568/CBP-9568.pdf
https://www.tortoisemedia.com/2024/12/04/715-million-spent-on-failed-rwanda-deportation-scheme

Dogs of War

Did you know that in Great Britain today
There are more rescue dogs
Than there are bi-pedal refugees?

And when it comes to our traumatised friends with four legs
We seek them out
We import them

They may bark loudly in distress
They may bite you too
But we must make allowances considering the abuse they've endured
And been through

Even if they behave differently and bark with strange foreign accents
To eyes visually impaired and deaf ears
Such nuance goes unseen, unheard

Unlike the herd of bi-pedals un-furred and unleashed
Climbing aboard inflatable boats chasing liberty and civility

Voting with their feet searching for release from their trauma unending
Searching for relief from journeys longer lasting than durations of some
quadrupedal life-cycles

If only we could all hear a dogs accent, would
they know the same welcome?
Or would they feel the same hostility and strife as bi-pedals of lower cast?

Cast off like flotsam, like spent effluent

By those passionately protective
Of privilege and affluence

Footnote:

PDSA.org.uk Animal Well Being Report 2024 / Pet Acquisition
Commonslibrary.parliament.uk/research-briefings/cbp-9981/
Breaking-Barriers.co.uk Refugee Asylum Facts 2024

Labour Shortages

There is an abundance of jobs
That need to be filled
Skilled and unskilled
As an essential thirst in the economy
That needs to be quenched

But entrenched, there is a dearth
Of British Citizens, indigenous natives
Who relate to, or are prepared
To fill the torrent of vacancies
That they've long since benched

Fists clenched
They stand eager to prevent
Willing foreigners invited
To quell the labour market latency
To seize job opportunities

Advertised by British Government approved
Employment agencies
Recruiting in home countries
Drenched in jobs
Abundantly awash

And oh gosh
Problem is, they are foreign
They are black
They are brown
And with that

Too many white Brits, ain't down

"Just got out the EU
To stop them doing jobs
We didn't want to do
Now come back with a plan
We'll approve and like
And is right
For us
Here

Oh dear
How hard can it be?
It's simple
And clear"

Forty Seven

Will 47 be their last democracy?
Is 47 presiding as the first ruler of a US autocracy?
For freedom, fake media is being cancelled - as is wokery
Enquirers and dissenters of the thin-skinned tormentor are silenced too

In this mockery, this hypocrisy of a stuttering democracy
The 47th is the greatest man with the grandest plan ever
To deliver God-like miracles that only he can

And expedite revelations in a tumultuous process
That only he can comprehend and understand
Even if MAGA methods mean being underhand
With insider trading that only 47 to his cohort can command

Is 47 presiding as the first ruler of a US autocracy?
Is America today still the land of the free?
A coveted title that America protected from sabotage jealously
For almost a century

Will America still be welcoming to visitors like me?
Or for some unknown visa infraction
Are the odds 50/50 for people like me
Of visiting a Federal Penal penitentiary
For a temporary residency unspecified in duration
In order for 47 to protect the hallowed nation?

Did the people not know what they were voting for?
Are they happy to lose their jobs and pay much more
For everyday essentials, significantly consequential

In the hope of receiving undefined promised potentials
Of Love, adoration and respect reverential
That only an orange strongman can be-get?

Did they not see what went on, on January 6th, 2021
When as the 45th, he wanted his presidency not to end
But to stay alive?
And in doing so, he didn't give a fuck
How many protesters or police officers died or were injured

As 47, he is implementing massive tariffs
Against his enemies, America's nemeses, and his allies alike
To renegotiate and ignite an amends

Except against that of his great, great friend Vladimir
With whom he seeks to complement, reset and adjust
America and Russia's relationship he must
Because Russia is a pure dictatorship
In whom the 47 can thoroughly trust

The 47 is sensitive, skin akin
To eggshell - fragile, yet mendaciously agile
And anything but pensive and sentimentally reflective
Unless, like Zelensky, you harm and break his shell
By daring to say no, even if reasonably so

The 47 will take you to hell with no concern or care
Who accompanies you there
The 47 enjoys being offensive and rough
Verbally threatening, aggressive and tough
Except when it comes to Russia, for them, he only has Love
Perhaps his good friend Vladimir has indelible advice to school and give

Like how to seize foreign lands like Greenland and Panama
And provide 47 with arguments to justify his game from afar

To try to do the same as Vladimir
Has done to Crimea and portions of Ukraine
On how the 47 can enter presidential Earth bound Heaven
And continue to rule forever and from democracy, America sever

Is 47 presiding as the first ruler of a US autocracy?
Forever to sever America from democracy?

Footnote:

https://www.atlanticcouncil.org/blogs/new-atlanticist/russia-was-spared-from-trumps-reciprocal-tariffs-this-should-change/

https://www.latimes.com/politics/story/2022-01-05/by-the-numbers-jan-6-anniversary

If We Capitalise

Imagine
I am at the heart
Of an international clothing consortium
Manufacturing, distributing, and selling
The highest-in-class of wears and couture
Across the globe in exclusive boutiques
Clientele unique
With a spending potential, exponential

If we capitalise and abide
By human rights and regulations
In our multiple manufacturing nations
We are making at least one hundred million
In profits year on year

But if we fully capitalise
And manufacture this gear
Under our rules and workers plights
And human rights
And governmental regulations
We do not hear
Care for
Or bother to adhere

Our profits year on year
At over three hundred million
Will be an easy path to steer

Let's analyse
And see if we fully capitalise
Is there anything here
For us to fear?

Alone - A Solitary Black Man

1.
It's early January.
It's two a.m.
I'm in a bar, in a ski resort, in France
I'm out with a number of people
Who I don't know well

But on this night
Out from our ski chalet
I wanted to go and get a breather
I'd been getting cabin fever

So now I'm stood alone
On my own, gathering my thoughts
I'm drunk.
Emotionally in a slump

You see, three weeks ago
My best friend died
And although no new tears
Were falling from my eyes
I was yet to stop weeping inside

Out for relief
From the weight of shock
And disbelief
Full-up with grief

This young French dude

Purposefully stepped into my view
He invaded my space
Abruptly breaking my grace

Accusingly he said
*"You placed your hands
up my Mrs' skirt."*

Bemused, I replied
"What. No I did not."

The dude lunged at my face
He wrapped both his hands around my neck
And began to squeeze
I was unimpressed, to say the least
Yet I felt obliged to reply in kind

Unsuccessfully, he tried to take me to the ground
Silently I stood proud, rigid and statuesque
I didn't fancy rolling around
And playing his game of ground and pound

Then two or three of his mates
Attacked me from behind
Jumping at my back, punching, and kicking
Delivering hammer fist slaps

They tried to take me off balance
And make me fall to the ground
Silently, I was proud, I stood tall
I knew I couldn't afford to fall to the ground
To get kicked around, my head a football

In shock, eyes locked on my first assailant
Arms outstretched
His hands wrapped around my neck
Squeezing at my throat
In a vain effort to choke me
I stood strong and statuesque

In retrospect
Channelling my Idrin, Jamie
You and me, we were family
It had been three weeks since you'd passed
But it was like your strength and energy
Made the difference that saved me

2.
As suddenly as the intense interaction began
My attackers all melted away

It was like:
Peace. An attack. A melee. An affray
And all of a sudden peace set in again

And so I was stood on my own
A solitary Black man
In a busy bar, in a ski resort, in France
Alone.
On my own

And then the bouncers came
With a new refrain:
> *"You. You need to leave our bar*
> *Now.*
> *You are causing trouble."*

I looked at the bouncers
And calmly said:
> *"I've just been attacked*
> *By at least three men.*
> *And you're telling me*
> *To go outside on my own*
> *In a place that I don't know*
> *To be attacked by them, once again?*
>
> *"You must be mad, if you think*
> *I'm walking out there, without*
> *the people I came here with."*

The bouncers tried to persuade me again
But then they stepped back
And ceased with their refrain

I was placid, I was alert but passive
Fostering a posture as I'd been
Before those dudes attacked me

Perhaps having seen
How that turned out
The bouncers decided against
Man-handling me out

3.
After a while
The people I arrived at the bar with
From our holiday chalet, assembled together
And we set off for our holiday home, together

And as we walked through the snow
The talk soon turned to their questions:
*"Lee, what did you do
to make those men attack you?"*

All along that walk
And even after we got back to the chalet
Our holiday home
The call and response remained exactly the same
*"What did you do
To make those guys attack you?"*

"I told you. I didn't do or say anything."

"But Lee, they would not have attacked you unprovoked."

Upset, I was choked.
For these people
Although they'd only known me briefly
Chiefly, all our time together
Had been pleasantly enjoyable
And full of a gentle levity

Yet they spoke up
And defended them, the other men
Men they didn't know
Men they saw attack me
And not one of them backed me
Or believed my version of events

And for the remnants of that holiday
An uncomfortable time was spent

Surrounded by people
Processing that attack

Full of grief for my Idrin, Jamie
He would have had my back
Over those that attacked me
But I'd been alone, a solitary Black man

And I just wanted to get back
Home

III. TRADGEDY AND INJUSTICE

Grenfell

Enjoying a quiet evening lounging
Living life, tranquil
Alone or with family, at home

Communities with much to be thankful for
An alarm sounds. The fire bells sing
A tried and tested protocol kicked in

Urgent attention had long been required
Requests from residents, desired
Were treated with contempt, with mal-intent

An Englishman's home is his castle
But this was deemed a concrete tower
A lair, left with little care
Filled with unimportant, multicultural, multilingual rascals
Occupying a most ill-fated of castles

A tinder box cladding
A nest of synthetic kindling
Cotton-wool accelerant
Akin to a flame retardant repellent

Warnings came
And warnings went
Unheeded

Indeed, warnings seeded
Were ignored

Gangster capitalists
Structural racists
Passive-aggressive, unrepentant, petulant
Managers of tenants
Letting them know their place:
As serfs and minnows

Residents with accents and multicoloured faces
Veils and head-scarves
And radiant varieties of traditional dress
That just did not fit
Whatever they were
They were just not it

Not one of them

Consistently complaints fell upon deaf ears, for years
On this particular day, by the time
TMO members arose from their sumptuous pits
They had their tenants mired in a myriad of shit

Reality hit

Hyperventilating, and gasping for breath
Their conscious inactions had led to innocent deaths

Residents forced to make momentous choices
Without precision
Eyes stinging for vision
Amongst flying embers
Choking inhalations of smoke
No rehearsal, no test
No try-out, no reversal

How many times did residents have to get dissed?
How many times were their concerns dismissed?
You failed to comprehend why your residents were pissed
How many opportunities had to get missed?
To prevent
This tower
From lighting up like a candle wick
Like a super high-phosphorus, water resistant match stick

A frightening inferno illuminated the night
For too many lives
In London's sight
Burned alive

In concrete
A grave was made
Where distinguished lights of life
Were extinguished
With no last rights

And then
The government discharged
An incendiary grenade at the fire brigade
For failing to break with protocol
For following their training
For standing tall
With tried and tested protocols

They blamed victims for lacking common sense
For following official instructions
From emergency call handlers

A tragic situation needlessly arose

Out of profits
Prioritised
Over safety

Of the innocent souls,
Departed

Plastic windows
And plastic-filled aluminium façades
Like phosphorus on a matchstick
Fuel on a candle wick
Waiting
To be ignited

It's hard to imagine
Souls dying for a dearth
Of consideration of consequence
Dying
For conscious
Inactions

For wilfully breaching fire regulations
For a recompense founded upon gross negligence

Responsibility
Resides
With parliament
The legislature

The common man's rule-maker
Rule-taker
Safety-net breaker
Refusing tenants, resented, the right to have a say

Executive power eroded and chipped away
Clipping
At the weight
Of what was once a secure safety net

For what?

For maximum cash-cow pounds and profits

Was it really...
Was it really worth it?

You knew it never was
And yet
No one paid

Footnote:

https://www.regulation.org.uk/ob-grenfell_tower.html
https://www.newstatesman.com/politics/2019/11/jacob-rees-mogg-says-grenfell-fire-victims-lacked-common-sense-obeying
https://www.london-fire.gov.uk/about-us/grenfell-tower-fire/

Two Child Cap

There is an ever increasing wealth gap
That warrants mandatory free school dinners
And the winners of the day
Back in 2017 saw fit to scrap
Third child benefit

In a quest for no more compassionate recompense
No more irresponsible wasting of resources irredeemable

Instead they introduced a two child cap
Accelerating the children in poverty trap
Exacerbating the continually widening wealth gap

And like a slap
They said the two child cap had to be induced
Because a universal benefit was just not fair

Because people who were fortunate enough
To have more were being forced, coerced
Into acting like they cared
Snared

They were obligated of their hard earned cash, to be relieved
Deceived to give up a share
Gifted as previous generations had generously done before
So that young precious lives could be uplifted

To be physically and morally strong
In stance, traditionally British

Rather than castaway
On to rip tides like Moses drifted

No more compassionate recompense
No more irresponsible wasting of resources irredeemable

For brighter futures for children
For the youth
The truth is evidenced in proof
That the two child cap is leaving children trapped

Like malnourished scraps, hungry and lean
Because the money isn't there
And keen, adults have become dispassionately mean
Dystopian, indifferent and cruel. Haters

Advocaters for a responsible hyper individualistic rigidity
A cynical society, inflexible, unbendable
Undependable and none-negotiable
Salting our precious Earth

Against any potential utopian acidity
To the alacrity of firm private equity
Hedge fund profitability
An orthodox efficient economic instability
Unsustainably unexplainably

No more compassionate recompense
No more compassionate recompense
No more irresponsible wasting of resources irredeemable

As passively young bellies rumble with the hunger

But there's no one to care or take note
Because these hungry little beggars are unable to vote

Aside from their parents, who are punished
Like a warning, as feral deterrents

No more compassionate recompense
No more than absolute minimal investments
In tomorrows generation
For extraction is the future
And this visionary pride
Is where the betterment of this nation resides

Not powerless parents denied means to remedy
The indignity of poverty, a rigged lottery of unfairness
And its impropriety foisted unfairly upon them

Impotent like a discordant alcoholic
Facing an unwanted withdrawal
and an instant sobriety, alone and unsightly

No more compassionate recompense
No more irresponsible wasting of resources irredeemable

On hungry mouths in the nest
Incessantly chirping to be fed
Only remedy to be found is being asleep in bed
Comatose or starved to death
With hunger stalking every fateful breath

Just thank God that they were born in this great nation
Of compassionate civility
Could have been unlucky enough to live

In a land full of un-British uncivilised criminality
Where life is cheap

Where there is no even handed justice or dignity
Where the system reeks of corruption
And is not transparent and fair
With open and honest and loving state care
Like this

Are We Okay?

We cannot only live in the greatness of today
Sometimes we have to understand why
Things are this way
And how we have arrived here with such attitudes
With platitudes of tolerance for hateful spiteful intolerance
Reliable undeniable

Whether enlightened or intransigent
Is it an apparent arrogance
To think that this period, this now
That this life on Earth is the Zenith
How this is the best that Humanity has ever been

To think that it is impossible for us to sink
Even if we have broken the delicate link
With Mother Earth and Nature
Upon which we depend
Leading to a scarcity of resources

A mobilisation of forces
For manifestations of right and just wars
Until the use of tanks and missiles
And Drones and artillery pervades
To sing long solos and choruses
Of concussive serenades

How have we arrived here
At the poverty and misery of the injustices
That we constantly see

Yet you and me we have chosen
Not only to live this way
But we have chosen to look the other way
Instead of stare head on into the glare of the unfair
And address the pain and suffering
That is abound all around

Homelessness, displacement and vagrancy
Is not consigned to history
It is burgeoning and it is growing
And given a degree of legitimacy
With victims granted an invisibility in society
And deemed somehow to be at fault
So we walk slowly and fast past them on the street
Without missing a beat

And we see caravans of the dispossessed
In states of undress
On our computer, TV, and tablet screens
Following natural disasters or after
They have been bombed out of their homes
Left to roam on macadam canals, pock-holed by shells
At the bottom of steep ravines
Surrounded by mountains of concrete and steel

Where fathers, and sons, and mothers, and daughters
Delicately pick their way and feel
As they scramble like ants
Their desperate bare hands compete
In the absence of machines
To dig loved ones free
Only coping by hoping to see them alive, once more

And we are okay
As their visible discomfort screams at us viscerally

Whilst the world is increasingly governed by kleptocrats
Democratic dictators, annihilators
And strong men maniacs
Who somehow need to be restrained

And are we, are we really okay?

Superior Inferior

You and your kind are inferior
Irrespective of the eloquence of any of your arguments
We are not hearing you, any of you
We came here to dictate, to govern, to seize and to take
To put it in the most common of terms
We are here on the make

All that we see here are opportunities
To fill our pockets and feed our economy, 28 of Deuteronomy
We are here now to strike fear in you with impunity
To make good on a new-found abundance of rewards
We are superior
You are subnormal
Inferior, and backwards

We are scrambling for Africa
Because we are God's chosen masters
We are your Lords

This is no longer your land
And it needs to be tilled and mined
And managed by our authoritative, and exploitative hand

You rag-tag band of scavengers
Ungodly savages, you are now our servants
You need to be subservient and obedient of our new rules
And orders and ownership borders

For this is now my land

This is now mine and Gods own country, 28 of Deuteronomy
Ruled by the British Monarchy, your Glorious Head of State

I command, I demand you show me the interior
So I can take aim and secure my claim
On all riches and resources

Worthy of the deployment of
Our Majesty's Armed forces
To divide, kill, conquer, and pillage
To divide, kill, conquer, and pillage
To divide, kill, conquer, and pillage

And where necessary, quell uprisings and resistance
With abundant native blood spillage

You must be subservient and obedient
To our new rules, orders, and ownership borders

For this is now my land
This is now Gods own country, 28 of Deuteronomy
Ruled by the British Monarchy, your Glorious Head of State

It is both foolhardy and surprising
For these savages to be uprising

They think their multi-millennia living upon this land
Gives them a claim to these sands, these soils, these forests
These trees, these lakes, these diamonds, this gold, and these oils
And all the abundant feasts within

Death to all savages

Kith, kin and tribes
You will pay with your lives
Should you try to resist the righteousness
Of white adventurers

Enlist, enlist planters and colonialists
Let us crush these savage uprisings

Resist, resist
Noble to peasant every Great Britain who emigrates
Upon arrival, shall be afforded High Status to navigate survival

And we were castigated, subjugated
Indentured in our own lands

We fought as braves
And countless bands and tribes disappeared

Deported we now know, enslaved
To die in foreign lands without graves

The lucky ones died, or committed suicide during ocean crossings
We saw acts committed not known, so depraved
Tortured natives
New found apartheid's divides

The wholesale instigation of another Black genocide
Black Holocausts
Divorced, erased, scorched from history

Belittled and lowered from view
With tired arguments anew

A tedious erasure executed
Ignoring our persistence, and our insistence

Relegated as long bygone
With no need to debate, educate, or reflect upon

Footnote:

https://www.theguardian.com/uk-news/2023/apr/06/the-british-kings-and-queens-who-supported-and-profited-from-slavery

Archives of Empire. Volume II . The Scramble For Africa, Edited by Barbara Harlow with Mia Carter. Duke University Press, 2003

Freedom of Speech

You talk of our right
to freedom of speech
yet you try to beseech
and muzzle my words

You talk about
freedom of speech
but deny genocide as genocide
seen, witnessed, and heard
as Genocide Convention defined

Palestinian Action
sprayers of paint
Terrorists Proscribed
yet for their actions
name the innocents that died?

Talk about freedom of speech
when trust is kneecapped
hijacked as villainous words
spoken token
as
whose lies?

Mental Help

Sometimes, people desperately need help
They are in the midst of a confusing crisis
And no matter what you do
You can't get them the professional help
That they need, in time

Alone, you can't help them
Or even contain them
For their own safety, or others
They are unable to see that they're unwell:
Vulnerable, and desperately in need

Self-destruction, self-construction
And perception of self
Can be very blurred lines, at times

Sometimes, when things are going horribly wrong
You can seek assistance
Only to find resistance
In trying to prevent
That which is thoroughly preventable
However regrettable

In my experience
The terms **Data Protection**
And **Human Rights** are one big joke
They are terms which are too frequently used
And completely and utterly abused
By authorities

When it comes to covering up
Their lack of proactive
And reactive interventions
To prevent
And Protect

America

America America
Land of the free

America America
Land of liberty

America America
The land of riches

America America
God blessed America

America America
Where incarceration is a growth Black people industry

America America
A thriving manufactured monetised privatised penal penitentiary

America America
Where incarceration swells corporate budgets

America America
Where citizens are brought before law courts
        And supermax sentences are sought

America America
Where justice is a process
        And proof of innocence is fraught

America America
Envy of the world

America America
The worlds richest freest nation
    With rules unwritten of racial segregation

America America
In a perpetual state of social fragmentation

America America
In an unacknowledged and escalating civil war

America America
Did you ask the first nations about your genocide before

America America
Successive legislatures have endorsed in laws
    A disinclination to help its poor

America America
Advocates the criminalisation ostracisation
    And the kicking of the asses of her own working classes

America America
Citizens carted off to prison for life without parole

America America
Where more state wealth is invested in the refinement
    Of solitary confinement holes than her populations health

America America

Where under eighteens are given whole life terms

America America
Where there's less people than there are firearms

America America
Where good people need more firearms
        To stop all the bad people from inflicting harms

America America
A nation lacking in compassion

America America
Where semi-automatic guns are an essential
        And certainly not a fashion

America America
Hate in your heart it burns

America America
For more white patriots you yearn

America America
Televangelists have God in the bag

America America
You're pissing on your flag

America America
You say it ain't respected America
        Yet you are the ones who rejected and neglected
And disrespected your own people

America America
Where only 3/5th's humans far less than equals

America America
Chocking the Brother man's neck

America America
For the sanctity of life it shows no respect

America America
You say you didn't know

America's most imminent danger
Even whilst being lynched fear and distress they didn't show

Heck America
What did you expect this fucked up shit show to become?

America
You can't make sense of what you've instigated and begun

America
You can't make sense of your present let alone your history

America
It's little wonder finding your way forward is nothing short
       Of a cloak and dagger mystery

America
Un-united dis-united in angered states of America
       The whole world is watching you

America
I hope that we are learning exactly what not to do

America
And that we won't follow and imitate you

America

Distant Dawn

I. ECHOES OF HISTORY

Ancient Aborigines

Stood with eyes raised on skies transfixed
Bare feet on warm red brown mounded ground
Connected to Earth still and perpendicular
Erect and particular on this perfect planetary prism
A spectrum of light splays and plays on solar winds
Floating like magma through mantle
Crystalline chambers and magnetic core
Internally controlled vacuum fission
In a galaxy on an unknown mission
Sailing humanity before stardust and meteors
Spun in gargantuan gravitations of a Sun
So smoothly and soothingly that we knowingly
Yet unknowingly only lust for man made chaos

At a loss and in contempt of the wonderment
The Miracle of the night skies before our eyes abound
Yet in nature a decline is found

But she is omnipresent and forgiving of us all round
Still providing invigorating and crucially, dutifully alive
Generously allowing us to share in theirs and strive
Despite Man unkind and his love child Capitalism's
Destructive lust for unnecessary needs to feed machines
Of automation and automobiles abundant
Until undesirably redundant
Like people proficient
But without efficient value to exploit discarded
And disjointed passports of national identities privileged
And therefore meant to be present presently worthy

In whom our so called leaders can trust

But if you could, would you just
Throw all of this baggage and garbage of today away
And follow the wisdom and teachings
Of the Ancient Aborigines?

Could you, would you see the greater picture
Of the minuscule yet numerous
And miraculous miracles
That we are constantly travelling through
A galaxies seasons, pirouetting perpetually
Without rhyme but for noble reasons
In and with, and amongst innumerable
Constellations of stars visibly invisible
Insignificant yet indivisible from nothingness
In it's vastness expansiveness of more than nothings
Light years of less

And ridiculed
They stood with eyes raised on skies transfixed
Bare feet on warm red brown mounded ground
Connected to Earth still and perpendicular
Erect and particular like antennas attuned
On this perfect planetary prism
A spectrum of light splays and electrons play
On charged solar winds discharged
As dominant and subordinate energies collide
Floating like magma colourful through mantle
Clear crystalline chambers and magnetic core

Grounded yet Astrally projected
Connected Ancient Aborigines soar

As too much of Humanity can do no more

1835

Great Britain
Once a global empire profound with subjects not smitten
Great Britain
A glorious history with uncomfortable truths neither spoken or written
Great Britain
when £20 million pounds was forty percent of treasury revenue
Great Britain
when £20 million pounds was five percent of GDP

In 1835 £20 million pounds was the sum paid
to compensate slave holders
the shackle and the chain owners
for the loss of their freedom
to gain, to restrain, to claim and to venture
in perpetuity to permanently censure
and indenture Black Lives

The ownership of me and mines
for unlimited and limitless millennia of times
my mother, my father, my brother, my sister
my grands, and great grands, and my children's

From 1835 until 2015, for one hundred and eighty years straight
the Great British Tax Payer being you and being me
worked hard and harder still to service that treasury debt
so that the slave holders could collect a state aid
A compensation that this ennoble nation
rewarded to killers and torturers
butcherers of freedom and their descendants listed in wills

who inadvertently remained our dependants
Freed not from their guilt, but freed from their ill
of rape, tyranny, ill-gotten gain
through whole human life larceny
depriving children and babies of their parents
and cheapening humanity to less than human
through their inhumanity for profit
called themselves plantation owners
and millers, but were really stone cold killers

How conveniently Britain
you sing about your Greatness
How conveniently Britain
you sing about your once Great Empire
How conveniently Britain
you speak of founding the industrial revolution

Well let me banish your illusion Britain
you did not do it all alone
We worked beyond our skin
we worked beyond our bones

The sugarcane toil of my ancestors
oiled mill wheels that received the cotton crop yield
from plantation field
hand picked from brown soils fertilised with my red blood
dried black and blended in the mud from skulls cracked
bare backs slashed from whiplashes hacked
for insolence unheard for laziness unseen, for just being
For being violated, for being raped, for being brutalised
For being sold and segregated, for being hot iron branded
For being me, for being we, for being us

And then for reluctantly agreeing to freeing
and being the beneficiary of one of the largest loans, in British history
In 1835 you were compensated by the treasury
for all the lives lost to you
In 1835 You were compensated for the liberty of the enslaved
now taken from you

And for us having to start over anew after lifetimes
after generations, after centuries lost to the barbarity of slavery
cast adrift at sea in the mist, without lifelines
You saw fit to give us a whole heap of something entitled nothing
No compassion, no compensation, no reparations, no hand not a leaf
just left ah strand in a strange strange foreign land
just left ah strand in a strange strange foreign land

Back into the throes of the former slave holders whip hand
for employment as share croppers
at his enriched impassioned and highly compensated command

Footnote:

https://www.bankofengland.co.uk/working-paper/2022/the-collection-of-slavery-compensation-1835-43
https://www.theguardian.com/commentisfree/2018/feb/12/treasury-tweet-slavery-compensate-slave-owners
https://www.dailymail.co.uk/news/article-2577312/Caribbean-leaders-sue-Britain-slave-trade-150-years-

A Tribute to the Forgotten Soldiers

In this country's hours of need
People of all races, religions, colours and creeds
Muslims, Christians, Hindus and Buddhists
Sikhs and Jews, to name but a few
Travelled from afar to perform and undertake
Selfless deeds for the sake of this Country, urgently

Irrespective of whether they trusted or liked her
Or believed in her causes and contradicts
That led to edicts of disputes to be resolved
By taking up arms, by fighting in wars
Of brutalist barbarity, unimaginable in totality
Until they reached their bloody eventuality

They travelled from their home countries
In multiples of millions and fought
With unpalatable bravery in the face of fear
In Africa, Asia, and here in Europe too
Sacrificing themselves to assist
And protect the global interests
Of this little piece of land called Great Britain

When the UK came calling in its hour of need
They could have put up their feet
Looked out on their fine and tranquil vistas sweet, and said
 "Your war, your dispute, your business
 Is nothing to do with me"
But instead, they bravely answered this nation's call
Their humble selfless dignity

Remains a lesson to us all

And lets not forget that countless in number to fall
Never to see the legacy
For which they had so selflessly laid down their lives
To benefit you and me, but were ultimately deprived

Would you reciprocate and do the same
In answering that call?
Or would your consideration be only for yourself
Above anyone else at all
Even if it was for the betterment of all?

II. FACES OF INEQUALITY

Black Lives Matter

Once upon a time
In the Americas, Africa, Europe, and Asia
Black and Brown people fought in the white man's wars
To reinforce, and reinstate your rights, your rules, your laws
So that you could gain more land
More wealth, more minerals, more wars
Or at least keep what you laid claim to as your protectorates
Territories and colonies

We laid down our lives amidst apartheid
Complex prejudice, and Jim Crow laws
Where forces friend to me
Were also my enemy

We wore your uniforms
Yet conformed to a far different set
Of tolerance, and norms

Once upon a time
Black people campaigned for Civil Rights
Just to be treated in a civil manner

And then we campaigned for Racial Equality
Asking to be given a fair chance
Equal in opportunity
And circumstance
To that of other races in all places
Irrespective of the shade of our faces
Not better

Just equal

And now
We have Black Lives Matter
Campaigning, pertaining now
To tell you
That we matter

Like those other lives
That seem to matter
Far far more than that of ours
When in the hands
Of those that have been entrusted
With the power
To protect, extinguish, or detrimentally affect
Ours

We have been, and are, perpetually vilified
In twilight
Caught between the scorching sun
And the night of the long knives
Which is extinguishing our bravest, brightest
And the most brilliant of our lives

Is this the fault of every white person? No

Do Black people, as the Global majority
Wish to do harm to all of the white minority
Due to our knowledge of these continuing atrocities? No

However,
It is right, and important
that these things be known

That they be demonstrably expressed
and vocally opposed

And the imbalance actively redressed
without hesitation
in an open on-going consultation
resulting in socially positive
all-people-equal dynamic legislation

White & Cream

Indigenous
White and Cream
Rightfully seen

Brown and Black?
Stand back

Brown and Blacks
Invisibly serve
Without being observed

Brown and Blacks
Essential
Yet profitably unseen
To keep the country sired as
White and Cream

To keep this country
White and Cream
Ethnically pure and clean
For the indigenous man
To comprehend, approve and understand

Conducive
Exclusive
For White and cream

Angry and mean
Whites and creams

No faith in their religion
Or even-handed principles
Driving fact-based decisions

Just whites and creams
With irrational feelings
Insidious, knee-jerk dealings

Whites and creams
Trying to place
Brown and Blacks
Only as numbers
Under glass ceilings

For Brown and Blacks
To be battered
Attacked
Pushed back

Taking The Knee

I was sitting with a friend
Waiting for the kick off
The ref's whistle blew
And we knew
We were just about to see
The players take the knee

And he, my friend
Proceeded to tell me
With this taking the knee
He was getting ticked off
It was delaying the kick off

I looked at him quizzically
And he asked me
>*"Mate, this taking the knee*
>*Don't you think it's a bit tedious?*
>*I've had enough of it now."*

I maintained a poker face
As I thought, wow!

I said,
>*"I get your impatience*
>*As this taking the knee*
>*Is delaying your entertainments*
>
>*But imagine a whole life*
>*Working without payments*

Imagine having no time to yourself
For freedom or entertainment

Imagine belonging to someone else
Longing to experience a freedom
From constant harassment
Abuse and tedium
That you've never had or ever will see

If you can imagine just that
A little scratch across the surface
And this taking the knee
Won't seem so tedious and bad"

III. GENERATIONS IN CONFLICT

Intergenerational Strife

The state has abandoned the young
They closed down all the youth clubs
Shut down young people's engagement hubs
And sanctioned against babysitters playing
Even stopped children straying in the mud

They turned the young against the old
Conditioned both sets to treat the other as threats
They said that young children should stay, and play, at home
And never roam freely alone, outside
Without always being under parental supervision

And parents now fear being despised
As bad and uncaring if they
Let their children wonder and play
In joy, in surprise, in bright sunshine, unsupervised

And adults, especially men
Even if they love children
If they are not related to them
Must maintain poker faces
And avert their gazes and smiles
So as not to be mistaken and accused
Of being paedophiles

We have a burgeoning anxiety in the young
We keep hearing cries in despair of
> *"Where did all these mental health issues come from?"*
> *"What on Earth is it, that we have done?"*

Why do the young not respect the old, or strangers?
When they have all been raised to stay away from strangers
And distinguish none apart, from the start, as dangerous

Yet our time from swaddled baby, in cloth lined manger
To kidulthood, to full blown adult, is brief
So we must restore in all levels of society
Good faith, good will
A sense of trust,
If just, a well meaning belief

And reopen youth clubs
Rebuild young engagement hubs
Unlock community centres
To avoid misunderstandings
To pacify dissenters
Before they become tormentors

Let us bring the young and old together
To celebrate their commonalities
For Love is the glue that binds us all together
So let us prevent intergenerational intolerance and strife
And let us prevent this suffering - for life

Roofs Over Heads

Amongst other things
The responsibility of co-operative democratic governance
Is to oversee a vision for the commission and provision
Of growing Treasury income streams

Instead of a system in decline that is bursting at the seams
The government must take responsibility for growth
In social cohesion, for good reason
And truly know that it can instigate, initiate, innovate, and facilitate
The delivery of strength, security, and opportunity for all

In answering Keynes' call for full employment
And a constantly improving state of national wealth,
Of public health
And a balanced housing mix for all its citizenry

Whether public sector or privately owned
Whether homes for purchase or for rent

It is way beyond time for the government to fully repent
And become a major landlord once again
In every town, city, village and district

To put roofs over heads, indistinct without restrict
From the cradle to the grave
To see all children sleeping safely
In heated homes with warm beds
Where whole families are able to eat
And be heartily fed

With secure roofs over their heads
We need not be holed up in hostels
Hotels or converted industrial units
Or one-room bedsits no better than sheds
Where a full generation of children have now grown
Without ever having known
What it is to live in a permanent home

And for that reason alone
We demand the conditions to thrive
To live out our lives with pride
And not be down trodden, divided, or hidden
Ridden over, rough-shodden
As the almost-died invisible
Barely indivisible
From the long forgotten dead

In the 21st Century
Must the right to roofs over heads
Still be left unsaid?

IV. CRISIS AND HOPE

My Dear Deer

Iridium lights dazzle bright in summer night's fading light
Like omnipotent meteor, or sudden sun appearing gargantuan

Without warning or gradient of radiance, for my dear beautiful Deer
Her sensitive night sight disoriented in fright, by light omnipotent

She takes flight, brake peddle is stamped, but panicked Muntjac
She doubles back, too late, for inevitable thwack

Slowing car and shocked deer collide. And my beautiful dear
She continues to slide along macadam surface, like ice

Adrenalin flushing her senses. In desperation she looks directly
At the lights reflecting in her eyes, full of surprise, pleadingly

She stares at us and tries vainly to get up. But she can't. And she shan't.
We alight car, the disorienting star, like aliens
emerge from craft in light shaft

My brother carries her to the verge and delicately lays her on the ground
She looks at us and whimpers struggling to breathe, as if asking for help

I stroke her soft coat and lay both my hands on her
I offer her love and healing and pray for her swift passing

I ask that this terrible pain won't be long lasting
My brother places his hand lovingly on her head

And I feel her heart beat racing faster and her body super-heating

As her organs begin to fail, and then, everything stopped

Peace set in, and her soul set sail
And we could not fail to be tearfully moved

We could not leave her alone by the road side
So I cradled her, and carried her up the edge of a field

Perpendicular to the verge, finding a row of trees to lay her to rest
A final act of love from loving humans, full of remorse and regret

For A Beautiful Deer, whom I wish we'd never met
So she could have lived on, untouched by trauma, now gone

For My Dear, Beautiful Deer
Fly forever, no longer in fear

Humankind, blind.

Can we learn to live with empathy and love for one another
And all life vital we are fortunate enough to know and find

We must be kind

Carbon Credits

Blooms of growth increasing continually
Plumes of smoke, produce gross fumes, toxic
Complex hydrocarbons, and industrial waste passes
Chemically heavy metals, and noxious gasses, though our skin

Inflated our lungs with polluted air are filled
Tastelessly ingested through our food chain
Deposited in blood platelets clogging arteries, and veins
Radical proteins welded deep, into our brains

Neurones misfire, synapses prematurely retire
Reprogrammed cells divide and collide
Confused, some cells go to war and commit genocide
And innocent children are meeting premature deaths

Because industry and transport tainted air
Means they can't draw fresh breaths
Exhausted plumes of smoke produce gross, fumes toxic

Earth's seas swell, bathed in plastic
Melting ice caps receding drastic
Methane released from permafrost lost
Fantastic glaciers rapidly retreating

Raw sewage released into oceans and rivers, without treating
Environmental heating, seating, greeting wild fires
Carbon unlocked in unceremonious funeral pyres

Hurricanes, tornadoes, supercell storms

About which we only learn to take heed
Once we've been flooded or burned
But about which we learned on-line, in real time
On prime time news

Through cacophonies of loudly arguing opposing opinions
Sponsored lobbyists' views and voices claim
The problem resides in you and your individual choices

In contrast, consciously, we are copiously jet-setting
Diligently off-setting
Our pollution, begetting solutions with polluting debits
Buying that wonder product called carbon credits

So how can it be that this is still a problem?
I have paid my carbon credits, wasn't that the fix?
Why are children still coughing up plastic bricks?

Footnote:

https://www.climateimpact.com/business-solutions/carbon-credits-explained-what-they-are-and-how-they-work/

Pay

Bring back weekly pay
Bring back the cash payroll
Bring back choice for people
And their families

To be tactile with their incomes
To see and feel their money, hard-earned
To choose how to use
Their milk and honey

Where in difficult times
Particularly for those
At the bottom end of the income scale
If budgeting and all else fails

To have security and comfort in knowing
They will have more money
In hand
In just a few days

Understand, this will give them
Greater autonomy, flexibility
Self-determination
And self-empowerment

In the convenience of ways
That people are able live
Each
And everyday

Bring back weekly pay
Bring back the cash payroll
Bring back choice for people
And their families

To be tactile with their incomes
To see and feel their money, hard-earned
To choose how to use
Their milk and honey
Letting dignity grow

Encouraging people stuck
In a financial hole
On the dole
Living in fear of surviving
A whole month without any funds

To re-enter the workforce
Safe in the knowledge
That there is a source
A weekly payroll

Working to their advantage
Aiding them to calculate, and resource
Happier as a productive member
Of a truly, mutually beneficial
Workforce

Upwardly cohesive
Heartily adhesive
Unified and tight
Right?

V. PERSPECTIVES OF LEADERSHIP

Decide

Some of my closest friends are white
And enough of them lean to the right
I understand
There are elements of their customs and culture
That they wish to conserve

But people like Trump, Farage
Badenoch, Braverman and Musk
They know only divide and cruelty
Their egotistic egocentric duty
Is to wreak havoc, harm, and rage
Dismantling revolutionaries on a stage
Where cruelty's the script and greed is the wage

Maybe, in their element
It's an evolutionary
Survival of the financially fittest

Preserving nothing
Salting the Earth
Draining dry the lake
Fraying and filleting nerves
Awakening new waves of destruction
Dismantling trust
Faith in truth
And purveyors of the Just

They promote the bitterest of attitudes
With no grace, no gratitude, no kindly hand

Because they can

But that is not the way
Only tolerance, empathy and acceptance
Inquisitiveness about one and other
Showing, growing, caring and sharing
Together
That is all that builds
A more trusting and loving world

Whether you lean to the left or the right
Whether you are black or brown or white
The glue, the love, the customs, and common threads
That bind us
Are far more plentiful
Than the differences that divide us

But it is you who must decide
To see our value
And choose
Not to deride

Arise From Your Slumber

Rise up, awake from your slumber
We are far too bright and numerous in number
To not be confident in our own rights and abilities
To live in the light and find ways
To make new days bright
And shine iridescent and ever omnipresent

Have clarity of sight, invoke and invite
My Black and Brown Kings and Queens
And all other human beings to arise
Meditate invigorate, and energise your soul
Formulate new goals, uplift our whole
Consciousness higher together

With an expansive intention and desire
Shout, extol and represent your scrolls, your scriptures
Imagine and paint aspirational pictures
Visualise positively in your higher mind
To actualise in this reality, and manifest
Truth, empathy, and sincerity in this world
Of linear time reality, physicality

Stand in your power and take the positive steps
To crush all fallacy, and fakery
Negatively perpetuating an irrational fear
Of harmony and love

Rise above irrational critics, cynics and foes
Could it be that they are statuesque and froze?

Just suppose that they don't want to see us soar

On our path of righteousness
That you, me, and we have set for ourselves, and chose

Rise up, awake from your slumber
We are far too bright and numerous in number
To not be confident in our own rights and abilities
To live in the light and find ways
To make new days bright
And shine iridescent and ever omnipresent

Emerging in the Light - with Insight

I. IDENTITY AND HERITAGE

X-Lee Poetry

X-Lee, you wonder who is he
X-Lee that's me
X-Lee

Am I using a moniker to hide my identity?
You may ponder, does X-Lee have so little pride in his name?
Is X-Lee a poet with a dearth of faith in his talent
In the delivery and reciting
Of the rhymes the he's been writing?

Well let me put you in the frame
Granted you may not care all the same

I was born Malcolm Lee Codrington
And like so many West Indians
Malcolm is used for formalities
Lee is used by my friends and our families

I had no idea, until as a child in the Doctors
They called a Malcolm in
And my mother took me, by the arm
To the consulting room
I'm surprised, eyes wide, boom!

My known name is in the middle
Lee, that's me
I am called Lee, most commonly
Lee, the three letters one
Lee, the third son of Lyrical Empirical Endeavours

Lee the laid back one
Always ready, to Let Everyone Enjoy
Lee meaning the protective meadow
Offering a shelter
Lee the provider of a safe haven
A sanctuary to rest most peaceably

Codrington is a given name
It originates from a village of the same name, near Gloucester
And although I've never lived or ever been there
I like to imagine the natives will foster me
As one of their own, home grown, sealed and sown

Codrington, a name given by Christopher Codrington
And his descendants, plantation master of colonial dependants
A master holder of the enslaved
From their cradles to their graves
Or bought, enslaved in the triangular trade
In Barbados, Barbuda, and Antigua

He bequeathed a legacy, constructed a library
Commissioned, built, and fully stocked
With journals and books
In which students studied and looked
Paid for by the proceeds
Of depriving people like me
Of their free lives lived at liberty
To succinctly put it all too very nicely
At Oxford University, in All Souls College
So the best of the best of British
Could acquire the knowledge

In the great year of his death in 1710

At Christopher Codrington's bequest
To the Church of England's missionary wing
A profitable Barbadian sugar estate was gifted, by him
And over three hundred enslaved labourers
To till and cultivate the Churches new land
With wearied and calloused hands
And by his Society for the Propagation of the Gospel (SPG)
Codrington College in Barbados was formed

When to prevent the newly purchased enslaved from escaping
Christopher Codrington was found demanding
He pioneered the hot iron branding of the word
"SOCIETY"
Across his bonded enslaved peoples chests
So that he could have certainty, and peace
In identifying where his investments would rest
Even if they tried to ever break free
He could put his bondsmen to absolute test

Let's put our hands up for a vote
After the words that you've just heard written as spoke
Is this a name that you would want to promote?
Take note and raise your hands, if you agree
If this is a name that you would proudly carry
To represent your integrity, within society?

My father named me Malcolm
After the man with an X
He actually wanted to call me
Malcolm X-Lee
After The Muslim Minister, Human rights activist
The inspirational, visionary revolutionary

Who was taken back from this Earth to eternity
Far far too prematurely
Six years before I was born

However, my mother intervened
Insisting my father dispensed with the X
But she reluctantly agreed to Malcolm Lee
And thereafter, Lee, she knighted me

Malcolm X stood for what he knew
He stood for what he believed
And when he was deceived he put in hard graft
And dared to break away from Elijah Muhammad
And cut his own path
Malcolm cared, he shared, and was a Spiritual Mentor
To a boxing legend in the making, Muhammad Ali
And he transitioned him away
From Cassius Clay
And to his last, Ali regretted the day
When from Malcolm he had turned away

Malcolm X
I am proud of all that he achieved
And all that he came to be
And would have been
Had he not left us far too early
His loss, was a gargantuan loss
To the growth and constitution of humanity

Another copper skinned King
Who could have changed the world

But I am proud to be unfurled

As one of the innumerable bearers
Of this great man's name

And hence why, I
Have Malcolm's X in my poetic campaign
For the same reasons
For the words that I am writing
Electrifying and reciting, and fighting wars
One day, on word-smith tours
X-Lee Poetry's the name
This ain't a superficial game

Footnote:

https://www.asc.ox.ac.uk/codrington-legacy
https://www.asc.ox.ac.uk/sites/default/files/2022-10/Scrn1_Intro_edit1.pdf
Roberts & Smith 2016, Blood Brothers, 309; Baldwin, Notes of a Native Son, 101;
Roberts & Smith 2016, Blood Brothers, 309; Ali with Ali, The Soul of a Butterfly, 84-85

Black

BLACK lives matter, Black
No longer will Black step back, Black
It's time for US to be LOUD, Black
About OUR achievements be PROUD, Black
LOVE OUR smooth Black skin, Black
Stand tall for YOU and ALL, Black
Hold Your head up high, Black
Raise Your fist to the sky, Black

We've been under attack, Black
Every day be more alive, Black
Uprise and thrive, Black
LOVE Your Black, Black
Others only see our Blackness, Black
They think We're devoid of intelligence, Black
They think We're devoid of ambition, Black
No surrender no submission, Black

They say We're over educated, Black
They tell us We're sub-normally educated, Black
They say We're over qualified for the role, Black
No one told Me I was over qualified, Black
When it came to digging holes, Black
No one told Me I was over qualified, Black
When it came to sitting on the dole, Black
No one had My back, Black
When wrongfully, I was given the sack, Black
No one had my back, Black
When violently, I was attacked, Black

WE need to take back control, Black
It takes a village to raise a child, Black
It takes a village to build a business, Black
It takes communities to provide opportunities, Black
Give Yourself permission, Black
To take OUR narratives back, Black

They say You can't deny history, Black
The truth is, they tried to rewrite it, Black
Thought the white world could oversight it, Black
They say that no one cares, Black
That We've been erased from OUR story, Black
Sugar coated, Black
Lashes with salted gashes, Black
Unrestrained abuse, Black
Negro brandings, Black

Master's sexual demandings, Black
Whip, shackle, and chain, Black
Written out of OUR immense history, Black
Is My bitterness a mystery, Black
I can never fully reclaim, Black
Or take back what they took from ME, Black

For millions and millions of years, Black
We're the evolution of humanity, Black
We are whole human history, Black
We seeded all religions, Black
Our melanated imprints are profound, Black
Found way way, way way back, Black
Carbon dated in fossils, Black
We're found in rocks and coal, Black

Black miseducations, Black
Black misrepresentations, Black
Black incarcerations, Black
Black castigations, Black
Black demonisations, Black
Black miscarriages of the law, Black
Black miscarriages of justice, Black
Summary executions Black

Policeman said he was scared, Black
Black brother and sisters dead, Black
Just because our skin is gorgeous, and melanated, Black
Black WE MUST push back, Black

Black Lives matter, Black
Black Lives matter, Black
Black Lives matter, Black
Push back with waves of LOVE, Black
Push back with waves of LOVE for that
BLACK

POWER

II. MEMORY AND ACCOUNTABILITY

Lest We Forget

Lest we forget the soldiers, the sailors, and the airmen
who had the strength and will to serve selflessly without relief
irrespective of their convictions, thoughts, or beliefs

Lest we forget the wives, the mothers, the fathers
the sisters, the brothers, and all familial others
who held their nerve

Lest we forget the needless political posturing
that led to the aggressive fostering, of war

Lest we forget the crude attitude to the vast multitude
of innocent lives lost to the ravages and savages, of war
labelled collateral damages and not people, as before

Lest we forget the torment of friends and families displaced, by war
and without a home no more
exposed to atrocities at a frequency, a velocity
they never could have imagined or comprehended before

And if you please
Lest we forget the refugees treated like a parasitic disease
instead of victims of terrible chance, and happen-stance

Lest we forget the present, past, and history
of what the Military Industrial Complex be-gets of all this misery
and tragic loss of life, and the rewards that IT serves to protect

Lest we forget and end all wars

through vanity humanity will keep on repeating this cycle
more intensely than the wars that came before

Lest we forget all life is glorious and vital
peace shouldn't be a privileged state in which to live
It's something to which we should all, be entitled

Leaders

Leaders
One day I pray that our leaders
Leaders, presently in title
And entitled

Will cease to be breeders
Of hate, violence, degradation
And war

We have to hope that one day, some day
In some way
They will wake up and become empaths
Whether willingly, or unwillingly

They will breath
And be stirringly bathed
In the pain and suffering
Of the people that have been slain

Upon their instructions
For human life line interruptions
Destructions
In the names of You and I

As empaths bathed
They will no longer be free
From being, seeing, feeling
And knowing

The torment of the torture
That they sanctioned
Saluted and advocated
In Our names to be executed

In the most diligent
And creative of fashions
By privileged devotees
And disciples of their regimes

With ingenious means to illicit
Visceral fear
Pain and suffering on suspects, traitors
And innocents alike

Empathic penetration, impossible to separate
Empathic sufferation, impossible for leaders
To distance themselves
And segregate
The misery meted out at their command

Like spectral hauntings
No longer an exclusive humorous vaunting
From which
There is no escape

Even Superman's cape, won't shield
And free leaders from this plague
Of the Damned
No amount of meditation

Prayers with soothe-sayers
Or sages

No more, will so called leaders be feeders
Breeders of hate mongers
Intimidators, killers and daunters

I pray for that day
For a new empathic consensus
A new conscious accountability
To bring an end to this conflicted senility

To bring about a new found civility
For we will all be amazed
When new enlightened days
Of generosity and peace pervade

And love, once again
Truly comes to town, and plays
And can be here to stay
And omnipresently be the only way

Until in our leaders
They hear seductive serenades
And their empathy once again
Evaporates and fades

III. AWAKENING AND OPENNESS

Embrace the Strange

Embrace the strange
Embrace different people
And cultures
Know that it is a choice
To see them as less than
Know that it is a choice
To see them as other than
Know that it is a choice
To only see them
As vultures and takers

As a stranger
When you see me
Walking down the street
Minding my own business
What do you see?

Someone subversive
Worthy of your abuses and curses?
Another immigrant?
Another less than?
Another other than, who to right here
This near, does not belong?
Reaching in and taking from
The hand of the working man
That which, I am undeserving?
Not realising that I am
A British citizen

And that You, Me and We
Are all of this world, irrespective
Essentially beholden
To this perfect planetary penitentiary
By chance
Neither selective or elective

Embrace the strange
Embrace different peoples
And cultures
Know that it is a choice
To see them as less than
Know that it is a choice
To see them as other than
Know that it is a choice
To only see them
As vultures and takers

So I am asking you
Again
To choose a better way?
To Embrace the Strange?
And dignify and magnify
The foundations for validity
Acceptance
And a love all encompassing
And omnipotent today, tomorrow
And everyday
For it is a far better
Way

Hearts

Sometimes
To be different
Is to be an enigma

To not fit
Or fall into expected stereotypes
Is to be a stigma

Sometimes
To be caring and loving
Because you naturally are
Is viewed as suspicious
As if your motives
Are nefarious and vicious

Sometimes to be generous
To be giving and encouraging
In others as the best ways of living
To advocate and be all for empowering
Is eyed with cynicism
And leaves you open
to criticism
As being opportunistic of devouring
Because of the rightful praise
That you have been showering

And in the face of such negativity
You have to quietly and passively
Stand in your power and positivity

And not be afraid and do not cower

For these are the strangest of days
Where too many of the simplest interactions
Have to be undertaken in codified, measured
Well-manicured and guarded ways
In the most sophisticated of societies
In this the best of realities
It seems that separation
And segregation
As a form of protecting people
From one another
Is the greatest of priorities and preoccupations

Yet the further we are all drawn apart
Our default position from the start
Becomes one of mistrust and disbelief
And societies own bearer of grief
And broken hearts

Let us all
Come together now
Avow
Loving and trusting in one another
Once again
And cease to live our lives secluded
Isolated and apart

Let us all live in the light now
Together
And open our hearts

Kindness

We all can be automatic
And mindless without ego
And at those times
We can be at our best with kindness

You don't need a degree
To be free and to be kind, you will find
Those who are awash with sympathy
Empathy and whole hearted integrity
Will have a gentle kindness
That knows no bounds
Of ingenuity

Kindness is an attribute that comes instinctively
From within
Like our instinct for Love
It is intrinsic and it cannot be learned

Your kindness is a skill of will
That cannot be earned
The kindness that you give, by some others
It may be spurned
But refraining from giving your kindness
Is never a good lesson learned

Kindness and character, the two are one
For kindness is the best of character
There are many factors
That may constitute a character

But where kindness is dominant
It is the main vernacular
It's omnipresent
It is living it is naturally giving

The importance of integrity and kindness
Could be compulsory curricular
For where kindness is dominant
It is the main vernacular

There is nothing more wonderful
Than the gift of your kindness
From one to another
However brief or prolonged

In that moment and for that moment
You are your kindness givers
Life dedication

Upon you, is the totality of their thought, attention
And consideration
Their active contemplation
Serves as a natural meditation

Your kind and gentle love of others
Manifests love in others
Your kindness is a perfect tonic
A medication to heal one and all

Whether near or far
In summer, winter, spring, autumn or fall
Your kindness unifies and brings us all together
Wherever, irrespective of climate or weather.

IV. VISION FOR THE FUTURE

Holistic Position

However and whatever may be
The perilous state of things
A better, brighter more egalitarian
And increasingly ethical future
Is not only perceptible, it is possible
And it awaits

But to navigate our way from here
To there
Requires foresight, will
And a diplomatic care and skill
To overcome the nay sayers, the shouters
And the doubters

To shine a new light irresistibly
Incandescent and Iridescent
To bring people with us
To embrace a new philosophy
Written and traced like a mantra
Indelibly imprinted
As a sacred prophecy

Just as the selfish idealism
Of capitalism was
And has been
This new philosophy, economic orthodoxy
And polity
Will be, has to be in opposition
To the abundant ills

Of laissez-faire capitalism
Whose failures and costs
Are born by the Public Purse
And ultimately
Wider society

As circumstances
Diverting gross governmental subsidies
In misguided priorities
Of corporations and private equity
As generators of National wealth
Health and improvers of our life chances

But whose
Profits resplendent are retained
Refrained from reinvestment
In hard times from businesses and employees
In their portfolios dependent
Deemed disposal commodities
Once essential and vital
Now lugubrious oddities

However and whatever may be
The perilous state of things
A better brighter more egalitarian
And a increasingly ethical future
Is not only perceptible, it is possible
And awaits

But to navigate our way from here
To there
Requires foresight, will
And a diplomatic care and skill

To overcome the nay sayers, the shouters
And the doubters

To shine a new light irresistibly
Incandescent and Iridescent
To bring people with us
To a place where every decision
Where every mission and every contrition
Must be, and will be taken
From an open hearted, holistic position

Master Your Destiny

To remedy this
To emerge from being submerged
In darkness to the light
Remember this

For we have to strike out
You are more powerful
Than you are led to believe
You have been oppressed
And deceived

By our so called leaders
Who are feeders
Breeders of misinformation
Based on a disinclination
To empower you

From a young age
We have been taught
To be good consumers
And to become ensconced

In elaborate chains of debt
To be-get an education
Elaborate chains of debt
To be-get a job
And a good career

Elaborate chains of debt

To be-get you a home
Elaborate chains of debt
To service those debts
That a good citizen consumer
Be-gets

Until time comes for a stone
To bear thy tome

But you are not limited
You need not be limited like this
You have the power to strike out and achieve
Anything that you wish
To positively conceive

But first, you must stand in your power
And believe in yourself
For you are a wealth
Of power and knowledge

You are a wealth
Of goodness and grace
You are splendid and blessed
If only you can break free of the stress
Under which you have been placed

To conform to the accepted orthodoxy
To accepted norms, even though
They cause alarm and harm
And we have been made to believe
That these are, inescapable

Yet you can create, and shape

A whole life scape
For yourself
For the betterment of yours
And our health
And that is true wealth

You are creators
You are your own innovators, originators
You can be free to be
The master of your destiny
And it begins with you

It begins with intention and will
And it begins in your mind
Put it out there
Seek

And kindred wild spirits
You
Will find

Better Tomorrows

We have to hope
That those who come tomorrow
Who are preceded by us today
Will be better than we are
In all essential, empathetic ways

They will know love and worth
In the simplest of all forms and things
That are shrouded in misjudgements
Of unworthiness
And considered worthless in this day

Kith, kin and kind
Will themselves come to know and find
What it is to be noble, and humble, and free
As their innate, natural, and intrinsic state of being
A state worthier than the elevation
Of any individual for achievements
Industrial or otherwise
For a prize, irrespective of size
That serves only themselves

They will know the reverence of equality
The sanctity and sanctuary
That all life should have and be
Unreservedly

For the sake of Mother Earth,
Gaia's greatness

And the harmony of Humanity
Vibrating on a frequency that honours all people
All elements of nature are vital and equal
Perpetually;

That intersects with insects, invertebrates
And all the birds flying occupying the skies
The fish and the plankton
The ocean's vast inhabitants
The rivers, ponds and lakes
And all land dwellers
Including the rocks and the soil
The plants, animals, and trees
On our beloved rare Earth

As she continues providing for us all
Increasingly and generously, unceasingly
Until we shamefully exhaust
Systematically extinct
Her precious resources

We have to hope
That those who come tomorrow
Who are preceded by us today
Will be better than we are
In all essential, empathetic ways

They will know love and worth
In the simplest of all forms and things
That are shrouded in misjudgements
Of unworthiness
That are considered worthless
In the misguided ways of this today

V. SELF AND COLLECTIVE HEALING

Essential Love

I have been the fortunate recipient
Of an abundance of love, healing
And positive energy
So much so that I know
I am very lucky
And for that I am very humbled

In times of illness and disease
The benefits of love in abundance
Leads in us to be found
An acceptance profound
Of that which we would not have chosen
But which we now face
With inner reserves
Of strength and grace

As a cancer survivor
I am very lucky
To have been the fortunate recipient
Of Love, healing, positive feeling
And the donation
Of a strangers kidney

In the throes of grief
They showed and bestowed
Upon me
A generosity unknown
To so much of humanity
An essential part

Of their loved ones life force vital
As family
To give me, a stranger
Another chance at life

That is consciously fortifying
Invigorating and electrifying
And because of their preventing me
From dying
Simply because they could
Without benefit of face-to-face gratitude

Or opportunity
To bask in the glory
Of being exceptionally good
But just because they selflessly could
For that I am very humbled
And I apologise
If at any stage on my healing journey
I grumbled

Even in the face of pain and disease
And considerations of mortality
And dying
All of which is in part
At the heart of the process
Of Living
Remember whilst you live
It is vitally important that you unselfishly give
Without sequester or judgement

Your love, your grace and kindness
Have powers that are profound

For there will be a time to be found
When your turn will come around
When you will need
The power of a strangers healing
And their essential love selflessly bestowed
Upon you
To help you prevail and pull through

Already Been

It is impossible you see
We cannot be all things to all men
We can only show parts
Of that which we are

We are like a constellation
We are like the constituent dust
Of a universe, a star
Shimmering and simmering in the cosmic breeze

We are not able to reveal our whole, instantaneously
But we can share parts of our complexity
Parts of the multiplicity of our matter
And that matters

You matter
And that which you show
Your daring to share is magnificent
Particularly on this day in this way
Where people sequester themselves
And stay away from one another

Be courageous
And allow other people, to know you
To get inside and feel your flow
For your facilities for growth, are majestic
Promoting new unique rhythms and dialectics
To break down barriers

Illuminate and shine
Enshrine new divine knowledge, on sceptics
New insomniacs awakened
From having previously been incurable narcoleptics

And once you get this
Once they get you
There is nothing you, or they can do
For once you have felt this proof
And seen and lived this truth
And been the glue
That binds and bonds us all together

You can not un-see
The Love you have already seen
In eternity forever
You can not un-become
What you are and have already been

So keep on looking
And listening
And this love you will be hearing

So keep on looking
And listening
And this love will be nearing

So keep on looking
And listening
And this love you will be seeing

So keep on looking
And listening

And this love in kinship

Will be now, and forever freeing

Kinetic Soup (A Prayer To Self)

There is no fear worse
Than the illusion of fear itself
There is no fear worse
Than the illusion of fear itself

Stand in your power
Stand in your power
In this and every hour

This information is not exclusive
We are all energy and ether
Conducting the conducive
We are all each and every part of this discourse

We are the kinetic soup in the Cosmic Sauce
We are three aspects of natures wisdom
We are soul, spirit, physical
We are the kinetic soup in the Cosmic Sauce

I like to be with my own thoughts
I am comfortable in my own company
If I can be at ease in my thoughts
If I can be at ease within myself

If I can learn to be at ease and accept the vastness
That only passivity and stillness
Can bring
In an ever changing and complex universe

I can experience aspects of the wonders
Of this world, and beyond
Irrespective of wherever I may happen to be
If I can comprehend and understand thyself

I will come to know the soul, spirit
And consciousness
That makes me perfectly
And imperfectly whole

And the pure kinetic energy, that is packed
Into this beautiful skin
And vibrating rhythmically
Within this biology

Yet linked to all and every piece of energy
Irrespective of frequency
By heritage, by evolution
By DNA, by stardust
By God

We are of and a part of all things
And all things are at the heart of Us
And none of Us can be apart from all forms
Of energy

We are vibrating at different frequencies
In a complex symmetry
So all life and energy is special
To You, Me and We

And however We may choose to live our lives
There a certainties to which We must comply

We have to eat, drink and refuel, recharge our batteries
We have to draw breath

We have to nurture and be nurtured
And We all have to face drawing our last breath
And experiencing our physical deaths

I am comfortable with the fact that one day
I must die
But up until that calling
I must keep on falling in Love
With this journey, this life

For at the time of such calling
It will not be an ending of all things
It will be a new birth, a new beginning
Of new love and learning
Where I will keep falling
In and out of new experiences

I will be carried by loved ones known
And unknown to Me
Who are fully acquainted with whom I am
More than I know myself
They will know what has made Me tick

Irrespective of assertions of any expert or critic
Irrespective of negative aspersions by any cynic
I will choose not to beat my adversary, ever with a stick
Metaphorical or otherwise

I will choose not to carry a grudge
Or harmfully judge, slander or bear ill will

Still if I can be wise
If I can be even and kind to all that I find
I can conquer anything that I put out to my mind
Nothing is insurmountable
I will always prevail and get through

It is not my role to know and understand you
But if I can be an expert on thyself
I'll have greater intuition and insight
Into what constitutes the magic of the universe
And what constitutes you
And I may be able to help or inspire you
Consciously or sub-consciously
Knowingly or unknowingly

Listen this true
Ultimately this journey
This life, these lessons to be bestowed
Are not just about me
They are about our interactions and intentions
With everything and all that is

So give of your best self
And enhance how others live

Give of your best self
And enhance how you are living
Give of your best self
And enhance how we all are living

And that which is Your best You
You need to keep on
Giving

Embodiment of Love

Be the living embodiment of love
And let your soul be illumined

Be the living embodiment of love
Ignite your light and let it shine bright

Be the living embodiment of love
Spread your love, and allow it to be mushrooming

Be the living embodiment of love
In all of your endeavours

Be the living embodiment of love
When times are good and rosy

Be the living embodiment of love
When times are hard, and you are on your guard

Be the living embodiment of love
When taking difficult decisions

Be the living embodiment of love
In times of desperate measures

Be the living embodiment of love
And every moment treasure

Be the living embodiment of love
And radiate peace, acceptance, and pleasure

Be the living embodiment of love
And empower those who enter your orbit
To come right in and absorb it

A Final Note

Quotations: *Wise words written and spoken*

"Power is like fire - a good servant but a bad master and the misuse of power is one of the greatest faults of any government, indeed it is a crime against the people" — Sir Donald Burns Sangster, Prime Minister of Jamaica, 1967

"I am no longer accepting the things I cannot change. I am changing the things I cannot accept." —Angela Davis

"You can't separate peace from freedom because no one can be at peace unless he has freedom." —Malcolm X

"Capitalism is the extraordinary belief that the nastiest of men, for the nastiest of reasons, will somehow work for the benefit of us all." — John Maynard Keynes

"Surely the day will come when colour means nothing more than the skin tone, when religion is seen uniquely as a way to speak one's soul, when birth places have the weight of a throw of the dice and all men are born free, when understanding breeds love and brotherhood" — Josephine Baker

"The word multiculturalism has become a proxy for a ton of British anxieties about immigration, race, difference, crime and danger. It's now a dirty word, a front word for fears about black and brown and foreign people posing a danger to white Brits. If you are an immigrant – even if you're second or third generation – this is personal. You are multiculturalism. People who are scared of multiculturalism are scared of you." — Reni Eddo-Lodge

With Thanks

Tony Rushmer. *Thank you profusely, for effusively sowing the seed and convincing me that this book needed to be written. Your encouragement, steer, and enthusiasm for the words on these pages were vital, and infectious. You made me believe in me. Above all, thank you for your friendship. Kindred Spirits are we.*

*

Robert Edwards, *a great friend, philosopher, lyricist and a rapper, with the most important of attributes - a voice. Thank you for your brotherhood, inspiration and your imparting of precious knowledge.*

*

Rachel Casson. *Thank you for helping me, in no small measure, to stay on the sunny side of the street. Thank you for being pivotal in manifesting transformation in my life, as well as in the lives of so many others.*

*

Simon Parr. *Thank you for your friendship, healing and support throughout my illness, and beyond.*

*

Cambridge Black Creatives and Allies. *Thank you for holding such a welcoming, wonderfully creative, and enriching space, where artistry and growth can flourish. Thank you for being guiding lights to doors of new creativity and opportunities, that otherwise would not exist.*

*

My Aunty Theresa and Uncle Dennis. *Thank you for being ever-present at a time when I was unable see the wood from the trees.*

*

All family, both near and transatlantically apart.

*

Mum - The five foot general! *Thank you. All that I am is because of You. You are a true force of nature and an Angel upon this Earth!*

X-Lee Poetry - A Biography

Born in Peterborough in the early 1970s to a Jamaican mother and a Barbadian father, Lee Codrington aka X-Lee Poetry has a Bachelor of Arts Degree in Music Industry Management. He lectured on the Recording Arts & Multi-Media Bachelor of Arts Degree programmes at the School of Audio Engineering, and thereafter, has spent the majority of his working life in the construction industry.

Writing has been a quiet passion in Lee's life that was never to fade, which was increased after receiving a cancer diagnosis. Being consigned to spending a few years on renal dialysis, awaiting a kidney transplant, Lee found great solace in writing poems, short stories and making music.

Lee has been writing verse and rhymes for decades, making passive observations and social commentaries of a world unfolding around him. These treasures were stashed in folders, cabinets and drawers rarely ever to see the light of day. Until recently when his friend and author, Tony Rushmer, enthusiastically encouraged Lee to publish this, his first volume of poetry.